HEALING FROM FAMILY TREE HERITAGES

ALSO BY GENESIS EDITIONS

Strange as it may seem, the family curse inherited by Oedipus at his birth has never been analyzed prior to this study. Going back four generations in the lineage of Oedipus, the author deciphers the transgenerational inheritance that alienates Oedipus until his discovery of his adoption and the identity of his parents. The crisis Oedipus then suffers appears to be a necessary journey for him to integrate his heritage, to heal and to be reborn.

The author shows why the cataclysmic ending of Oedipus the King, contrary to popular belief, is not a fatal outcome but rather a necessary ordeal which the hero must live through. The tragedy then becomes a catharsis

The Ancients already knew the therapeutic potential of the family links between generations that we rediscover in modern transgene - rational practices. Far from being a new fashion, the recognition of transgenerational processes dates back to the first shamanic type of communities. Their methods to cure "The Ancestor Syndrome" offer to contemporary therapies essential historical references and valuable teachings.

With the contribution of specialists from diffe - rent backgrounds, this collective book presents a wide spectrum of perspectives to bridge traditional and modern knowledges.

Tony Thierry Gaillard

HEALING FROM FAMILY TREE HERITAGES

How to Recognize and Work on Transgenerational Trauma, Patterns, and Other Burdens

GENESIS EDITIONS

By the same author,

- *A Model for Healing Family Curses, Oedipus' journey from outcast to hero of Colonus,* 2024
- *Shamanism, Ancestors and Transgenerational Therapy,* (collective book), 2020.

And in French:

- *Intégrer ses héritages transgénérationnels*, 2024 (7th Editions).
- *Thérapie transgénérationnelle et psychogenèse du sujet*, 2021.
- *A propos de la métamorphose d'Œdipe en héros de Colone*, 2020.
- *L'autre Œdipe, De Freud à Sophocle*, 2013.
- *Sophocle thérapeute, La guérison d'Œdipe à Colone*, 2013.

Author's website: www.t-gaillard.com/en

Cover: *Rebirth Cycle* from Elizabeth Lyle
with the artist's kind permission

Original French title:
"Intégrer ses héritages transgénérationnels"

Genesis Editions
Château Banquet, rue de Lausanne 94
1202 Geneva, Switzerland
www.genesis-editions.com
2nd edition (modified) 2024

ISBN: 978-2-940540-42-6

Content

Preface

This book is intended for those who wish to understand transgenerational dynamics, therapy and integration. It is the English translation of my French book, “Intégrer ses héritages transgénérationnels”, which summarizes twenty years of practice and research that I have presented in several French books for both professional and public audiences.

The purpose of this book is twofold: first, it aims to help readers become more aware of the importance of transgenerational links, and second, it presents an integrative approach that synthesizes ancient and contemporary practices—referred to as “Transgenerational Integration”, “Transgenerational Analysis” or “Transgenerational Therapy”. In my perspective, working through transgenerational inheritance is a learning and integrative process, a qualitative shift towards oneself.

Since transgenerational integration deals with the unconscious, it automatically belongs to the more general domain of Depth Psychology, which should be related to the ancient teachings and initiations. Thus, unlike other transgenerational approaches, which paradoxically do not integrate what they are historically grounded in, my analysis refers to ancient wisdom, simultaneously renewing it and enlarging the field of contemporary Depth Psychology.

This book would not have been possible without my clients, whom I sincerely thank for agreeing to share their experiences. Finally, I would like to express my gratitude to those who participated and helped to translate this work: Carolyn Trine, James Spears and Camille Pernollet.

Tony Thierry Gaillard, July 2024.

Become such as you are,
having learned what that is.
Pindar (518 BC – 438 BC)

Introduction

Unfinished stories have a surprising tendency to repeat themselves, as if destiny were urging us to understand them better. For once we understand their true meaning, we can integrate these stories and stop repeating them. Only then can we turn a page of our history and start a new chapter in our lives. This principle can be observed not only at the individual level, but also on a larger, familial and collective scale. In the words of Winston Churchill, "those who fail to learn from history are doomed to repeat it."

There are good reasons why things seem to repeat themselves. And as we will see throughout the book, recurring stories and patterns may well echo unresolved histories that live in us unconsciously and that we need to become aware of. Otherwise, without an appropriate introspective work, we can forever be confronted with the same dead ends, or with inextricable and recurrent situations. To help us find the roots and meaning of theses repetitions, today, transgenerational analysis comes as a fantastic support for introspective work. It considers individuals beyond their short history, integrating them into a broader temporal perspective. As the many examples in this book show, we now understand that some of our problems cannot be properly addressed without broadening the timeframe perspective, which reveals how some of our problems are linked to the unfinished stories of our ancestors.

For example, a father can pass on to his children the psychological consequences of a war trauma, and a full lineage can inherit the consequences of a family secret. Similarly, a whole community can pass on to the next generation its unsolved issues and burdens. This can happen with ecological debt from land pollution, where previous generations were unaware of the issue or chose not to address it, leaving the problem for future generations to resolve.

Here is a first example from my therapeutic practice in transgenerational analysis. Ever since she was a child, Caroline could not bear to be in a room when the door was closed. At work, at home or even in public places such as lavatories, Caroline had to keep the doors open to manage her anxiety. To help her, we started to work on her family tree. There, the unfinished stories concerning her parents and grandparents started to come to light. One day, she arrived highly excited and relieved as she told me that her issue with closed doors was finally resolved! Her mother had just told her that when she herself was little, her own mother (Caroline's grandmother) would systematically lock her in a room in their apartment as a punishment. For Caroline's mother, these punishments produced emotional trauma in the form of despair and feelings of abandonment. Caroline told me, "While my mother was telling me this, not only did I finally understand why I was so afraid of closed doors, but I also felt a physical change, as if something was evaporating from me. Indeed, without even thinking about it, that same night and the days after, I closed the door to my bedroom and to other rooms as if it had never been a problem! Since then, I haven't had any more problems with closed doors!"

I can't even begin to think of the number of people who, like Caroline, could benefit from having their parents and grandparents explain their difficult stories to them. If these events are not brought to awareness, later generations may be confronted with the same problems of possible transgenerational origin without knowing that they might have been passed down from previous generations. It is only in hindsight that such things become obvious.

Of course, Caroline had previously worked on her fear of closed doors in other therapies, and she was ready for healing. However, only a transgenerational analysis, and the attention that we brought to her family history, allowed her to discover the meaning of her problem. This confirms what Depth Psychology[1] has understood for over a century: giving meaning to one's symptoms remains the core requirement for healing once and for all.

Consequences of incomplete mourning

In an article as part of our collective book[2], Salomon Sellam describes a particularly interesting situation. A young girl named Aurélie, age six, presented symptoms of asthmatic bronchitis. Her father went to Doctor Sellam to find a solution for his daughter. In the discussion, he began talking about thc disappcarancc of his own father when he was only seven years old. Trembling with emotion, he described, with Aurélie by his side, how his father had committed suicide by asphyxiation with gas. Given the intensity of his emotion and how difficult it was for

---

[1] At the beginning of the 20th century, Depth Psychology qualified all the approaches integrating the unconscious. They then split because of theoretical dogmatic conflicts, and Freudians reserved the right to the term "psychoanalyst."

[2] Salomon Sellam (2020), « Le transgénérationnel dans les maladies pulmonaires » in *Exemple d'intégration transgénérationnelle*, Genesis Editions, Geneva.

him to talk about, it was clear that he had never fully mourned the death of his father.

As Salomon Sellam wrote, "Unsurprisingly, all these unspoken and unintegrated feelings have led the child to develop psychosomatic symptoms. She has involuntarily inherited a difficult family history, and her pathology reflects her unconscious heritage, all that has never been spoken about. To speak the truth without feeling that its content is taboo is the first step towards a reconciliation. Such a reconciliation will erase the build-up of negative emotions that underlies their transformation into psychosomatic symptoms. Aurélie no longer needed to show her parents that she has unconsciously taken on their problems by exhibiting asthmatic symptoms. The next stage was very simple: anti-asthmatic medication proved very efficient and after six months she stopped taking her medication." This example shows how unfinished mourning, like Aurélie's father's can lead to the development of pulmonary symptoms, which were an unconscious referral to her grandfather's asphyxiation by gas.

When considering the transgenerational inheritances of unfinished mourning, Serge Tisseron[3], following the work done by Nicolas Abraham and Maria Torok, talks of a "ghost therapy." In "*The Ghosts in the Family*"[4], literally Bruno Clavier also looks at the impact that parents' incomplete grief has on their descendants. Suicidal attempts and, according to Maria Torok[5], panic attacks, are manifestations of the presence of an unconsciously inherited

---

[3] Serge Tisseron (1995), *Le psychisme à l'épreuve des générations : clinique du fantôme*, Dunod, Paris. Serge Tisseron (1996), Secrets de famille, mode d'emploi, Ramsay, Paris. Jean-Claude Rouchy (2001), *La psychanalyse avec Nicolas Abraham et Maria Torok*, Éditions Érès, Paris.

[4] Bruno Clavier (2013), *Les fantômes familiaux*, Payot, Paris.

[5] Nicolas Abraham and Maria Torok, *The Shell and the Kernel: Renewals of Psychoanalysis*, 1994, University of Chicago Press.

ghost. That is why, it is important, when doing transgenerational therapy to identify in the family tree where there could be "skeletons in the closet" and clarify their lives as well as the circumstances of their death.

On the consequences of incomplete mourning, Marc Wolynn recalls the story of Jesse, a young man who had suffered from insomnia for over a year. "He was a star athlete and a model student, but his lack of sleep had initiated a spiral into depression and despair. Consequently, he abandoned his studies and quit playing sports. In just one year he had consulted three doctors, two psychologists, a sleep clinic, and a naturopath, all without success. His problems began just after his nineteenth birthday. His body became ice cold. Shivering, he was unable to warm himself up, and he felt seized by a strange fear that he had never experienced before. He was afraid that something awful would happen if he let himself fall asleep again, "if I go to sleep, I'll never wake up." Wolynn recalls, "every time he felt himself drifting off, the fear would jolt him back into wakefulness. The pattern repeated itself the next night, and the night after that. Soon insomnia became a nightly ordeal. Jesse knew his fear was irrational, yet he felt helpless to put an end to it." [6]

One bit of information stood out for Wolynn, that of the sensation of cold and feeling as if he were about to freeze. He asked Jesse if anyone in his family had ever had a traumatic experience involving "cold" or being "asleep." Jesse then remembered that his mother had recently spoken of the tragic death of his uncle, whom he had never known. This Uncle Colin was nineteen years old when he died, frozen in a winter storm when checking the power lines in Northwest Canada. He was found dead from hypothermia. Traces in the snow showed that he had been struggling to hang on to the power lines. For Colin, letting

[6] Marc Wolynn (2016), *It didn't start with you*, Viking, New York.

go meant dying. It was a tragic loss, and the family had never spoken of him since. Jesse who was the same age as his uncle, was unconsciously experiencing the non-integrated story of his family, and dealing with the same fear of letting go. The association between his symptoms and his uncle's death was a turning point for Jesse. He finally understood what had brought about his fear of sleeping, and he was able to begin healing. Not only was Jesse able to free himself of his insomnia, but he was also able to reconnect with his family, both past and present."

This last point is also interesting. When beyond the problematic history of his family tree, a client reconnects with more ancient family member, for example recognizing similar characters, or qualities, the therapist understands that the integration process has advanced, and that the client is beginning to see the light at the end of their therapeutic journey. I'll be developing this aspect in later chapters, but for now, let us simply understand that transgenerational analysis is not only effective for healing symptoms. This analysis also helps us to reconnect with our origins, which I also call the forces of life, that is to say with the vital forces of life operating here and now.

An unconscious transmission

Surprising as it may seem, we need to understand that unfinished stories do not just evaporate into thin air. When we repress or forget these kinds of stories, it does not mean that they are finished or that we have dealt with them. On the contrary, they are more likely to be transferred onto the next generation because of the efforts to suppress, deny, or forget them. These unfinished stories make up a "past that is not past", like a debt that will have to be paid one day or another. Transformed into something unconscious, these unfinished stories also become timeless by remaining suspended, and they hide behind all kinds of symptoms present in later generations. Since people are rarely conscious of the transgenerational origins of their problems, they may very well transmit them onto their own children.

Through many examples, we shall see how similar and symbolically related problems are found over several generations. It is as though our ancestors were asking us to solve these unfinished family stories more effectively for ourselves, and for the sake of future generations.

Strictly rational minds may doubt such a transmission of unfinished stories between the generations, yet the idea is not new. On the contrary, it goes back very far in the history of humanity. The ancient Greeks for example, were fully aware of such transmission across generations. For them, families were bonded together by blood, and they formed distinct units in which the later members inherited material goods, as well as unfinished stories from their ancestors. As we shall see in the second chapter, it is one of these traditional forms of knowledge that our modern civilization has lost. But today, this knowledge is gradually being rediscovered.

More than thirty years after the first transgenerational analyses, epigenetic research shows how much our heritage can influence our DNA. For example, it has demonstrated an increased vulnerability to stress in descendants of Holocaust survivors.[7]

Epigenetic evidence of the transgenerational

Biologists measure the importance and complexity of that which is perpetuated by way of blood and DNA ties. Their research indicates the presence of transgenerational consequences when ancestors have suffered trauma or

---

[7] Yehuda, R, Schmeidler, & al. T. *Vulnerability to posttraumatic stress disorder in adult offspring of* Holocaust *survivors*. Am. J. Psychiatry, 1998 ; 155 : 1163–1171.

other extreme living conditions. For example, descendants of people born to parents who experienced the famine of 1943-1944 in Holland are significantly more obese[8]. Another research has shown that negative experiences and fears[9] can have a long-lasting impact. It showed that they can leave their marks over several generations. It would be interesting to delve deeper into the subject to better understand the importance of somatic manifestations in relation to a person's ability to recount their transgenerational history. Individuals who ignore the unintegrated stories of their ancestors might be the most affected. In contrast, those who have been able to engage in transgenerational integration are more likely to develop a stronger immunity against potentially pathogenic genetic heritages.

These epigenetic discoveries have liberated significant financial resources. However, if psychological factors are neglected, then their therapeutic applications will be limited. If we do not recognize ourselves as the primary actor in our healing, we risk losing the use of our own potential as a source of resilience, and we may become more and more dependent on mere provisional solutions, such as a palliative, medical, digital, or robotic interventions, to deal with growing and persistent problems. Indeed, traces left in our DNA by certain life experiences depend on the way these situations have been responded to. As we all know, people will react to similar experiences in different

---

[8] Marine Courniou, « Nos états d'âmes modifient notre ADN », *Sciences et Vie*, 1110 (03/2010), Paris ; Veenendaal M, & al. *Transgenerational effects of* prenatal *exposure to the 1944–45 Dutch famine*. BJOG 2013; 120 :548–554.

[9] Katharina Gapp & al. *Implication of sperm RNAs in transgenerational inheritance of the effects of early trauma in mice*, Nature Neuroscience 17, 667–669 (2014).

ways. In these future epigenetic medical treatments subjective and personal transgenerational integration could make a difference in terms of sustainable healing.

Reconnecting with our roots

Nowadays, because DNA testing has become so accessible to many people, gathering information about our ancestors is a far less challenging task. The success of DNA tests also reveals a deep desire to know where one comes from in broader terms, and indeed, it can reveal the identity of unknown relatives. This is important because the more we ignore the history of our ancestors, the greater the risk of inheriting their unfinished stories.

In that perspective, unveiling our transgenerational heritance helps us to understand how much our relationship with the world, and our way of life, are unconsciously conditioned by our family and culture.

In our world of profound changes, transgenerational analysis meets today's therapeutic needs. Faced with the risk of over-adaptation to the virtual world, transgenerational integration offers the possibility to restore a certain balance. In this context, the rediscovery of transgenerational principles comes right on time to invite us to come back to ourselves and to integrate our roots, so that we can better understand where we come from, where we stand, and where we are going.

Today, we only begin to recognize the importance of what is passed from one generation to the next. Thanks to transgenerational analysis, we know that what our ancestors were not able to integrate such as traumas, secrets, and emotional burdens can become unconscious heritages. These can continue to be handed down to future generations unless they are dealt with, hence the term "transgenerational", used to qualify these types of inheritances.

In addition to observable forms of heritage (morphology, material goods, talents, skills, *savoir-faire*, etc.) therapeutic experiences have taught us about the existence of "invisible" transmissions, associated with non-integrated events and conflicts that once belonged to our ancestors.

In accordance with the admitted vocabulary, we need to clearly differentiate between ***intergenerational*** transmissions that are voluntary, conscious, and verbalized, and ***transgenerational*** transmissions that are unconscious, nonverbal, involuntary, and potentially pathological. While intergenerational activities support exchanges between the generations (in a constructive and preventive way), transgenerational dynamics pass on problems to the next generations without them even realizing it.

We are not just a result of our past

In the face of this historical predetermination, the question of self-knowledge, that is, of our true Self, is essential. As I will develop it in my analysis, it is the Self that lies at the heart of the integration processes. *Actually, the Self is that part of oneself that is tied to the present moment, from where we can integrate the "past that is not past", rewrite it, and recapture it.*

One consequence of transgenerational unconscious heritages is to render us alien to ourselves, to drive us away from ourselves. It always starts with a difficulty to be one's true Self. If unintegrated the unconscious forces will operate despite our best intentions and will make us less authentically ourselves. From an etymological perspective, "alienation"[10] is the term which best describes this process of losing oneself. It is derived from the Latin *alienure,* "make other" or "make stranger" to oneself. It refers to a "state in which human beings are somewhat detached from themselves," and in a more general sense, to

---

[10] See the complete definition of alienation in the glossary.

the "loss of one's authenticity." "I am another," said Rimbaud, to signify that one can be alienated by someone other than oneself, by an unfinished story tied to our family or to our culture. Most of the time we are not authentically ourselves, but rather, we are conditioned by our education, and we adapt to our surroundings. Freud also shared that idea, "the Ego is not master in its own home."

More specifically, integration work focuses on bringing to light the unconscious (or our dark side), so that the Self in us can be given a place. Certain psychological schools of thought also talk about "sub-personalities," which are not to be confused with the true Self. For Jung, "fulfilment has no other goal than to release the Self from the false envelopes of the persona."

As we shall see, because it is rooted in the present moment and independent of time, the true Self has the quality of being unalienable, irreducible to any past events. It exists in the present time, in the flow of life, which connects us to the sources of the living. In a more symbolic language, I also call it the origins. These are not to be found in some ancient time, but beyond time, in a timeless symbolic dimension, like the unconscious. In other words, it is in the present moment that our Self meets the forces of life which are inseparable from our origins. However, most of the time, the Self is unconscious and left in a potential state, waiting to take place. This is why the Ancient Greeks exhorted us to discover that part of ourselves that is essential: *Know Thyself*!

With transgenerational analysis, unveiling what lies unconsciously inside us also simultaneously reveals the presence of a true Self waiting to befall us. In other words, becoming aware of our alienations is a first step towards becoming our real Self, towards that inalienable part of ourselves that can integrate its prehistory. Explanations are not enough to achieve this but may constitute a first step to integration. Here, the support of a transgenerational analyst will make the difference to help integrating transgenerational heritage. As I will develop it in the last chapter, the "par excellence" analysis of the unconscious remains that of a hermeneutic of the Self, a way of recognizing what is not visible at first.

Once we become aware of these legacies, the ways in which we react to them will naturally change. By differentiating what alienates us from our authentic Self, a process of becoming our real Self can begin. As we shall see in the following examples, it is then possible to have a positive impact on symptoms and other existential problems.

1
Roots' Stories

Every birth is a story that begins well before the day of delivery. We do not come to life from nowhere. The personal, material, and cultural conditions of our parents and families have already influenced the circumstances of our conception and birth. Was it an "accident"? Did it happen at a difficult time? Has the family recently suffered a loss? Were the families of both parents encouraging or hostile? Were they present or absent? What do we truly know about our prehistory, and to what extent does it connect us with the stories in our roots?

As I have observed many times in therapy, when people begin to pay more attention to the history of their ancestors—beyond just their direct connection to their parents—their resistance to confronting their own past starts to diminish. Expanding the reflection across multiple generations reveals new perspectives that help patients better understand their own stories. They discover a new way to analyze personal episodes that were previously overlooked, allowing them to put words to nearly forgotten pains. In a way, the ability to talk about transgenerational history satisfies a natural desire to clarify our patrimony, to free one's Self from hidden heritages, and to transmit a positive intergenerational heritage.

With the transgenerational approach, parents are more likely to talk about their lives, recalling childhood memories as though they finally dared to put words onto difficult experiences that have forever lurked in the back of their minds. Moreover, when death knocks at their door, people often feel the need to reveal their secrets, hoping that this could provide them with a sense of peace. Some people also feel the need to ascertain their genealogy, when for example, they are unsure of their paternity. However, what they may not realize is that by clarifying these unknowns, they also leave behind a tremendous gift for their descendants.

Unfortunately, our modern culture rather encourages us to keep up appearances as opposed to being transparent about our true stories. Consequently, instead of parents passing down their real-life stories and revealing family secrets to their children, they often bequeath them with material goods. However, if these heritages serve the purpose of hiding secrets and repressing guilt, they turn into poisonous gifts. Listening to my clients, I have come to realize that big material inheritances can be alienating for descendants of wealthy families. Caught up in unconscious conflicts of loyalty, they are often victims of heavy secrets that betray the reality behind the appearance of glamor. Here too, verbalized transmission and conscious legacy is of the greatest importance.

When these transmissions are lacking, we need to find in ourselves the appropriate resources to assimilate our prehistory. This is where we all can count on our true Self to integrate our transgenerational heritages. This is the meaning of the Greek poet Aesop's famous saying, "Help yourself and the sky will help you!" In other words, "wake your true Self and life forces will participate." Indeed, if transgenerational integration brings remedy to the lack of transmissions, it can also, as we shall see, put us back in touch with the forces of life, our origins, traditionally symbolized by the Father Sky and Mother Earth.

The consequences of a family secret

Here is an example that shows the impact a family secret had on another client of mine. Delphine asked for help to deal with a family secret that had had devastating consequences for her. After her divorce from a miserable marriage, one family member revealed to Delphine that her father was not the biological father of her eldest sister Arlette. When Delphine asked her father about that secret, he explained, "When your mother was pregnant, she went to her priest to confess, and then we got married anyway. But she was haunted by shame and guilt for the rest of her life, so that when your sister Arlette passed away, your mother screamed out, 'God is punishing me!'"

Discovering her mother's secret had been a shock for Delphine because she finally understood why her mother had forced her to marry the man who had just gotten her pregnant. Delphine had to obey, even though she did not want to get married and felt she was too young. Upon discovering her mother's secret, Delphine understood that she had been obliged to do what her mother had not done and marry the man who had gotten her pregnant. Her mother's guilt had forced her into an unwanted marriage. "By getting married, I re-enacted my parents' secret, I couldn't say, 'No, I don't want to get married,' it's unfair, it's monstrous. When I got married, I was a party to their secret at my own expense, by making my mother's unfinished story visible. I always told myself that I was living my life inside out, that the cards I had been dealt were scrambled. On the day of my wedding, I felt like everyone was present except for me... now I must make peace with what I have found out..."

By going back several generations, our transgenerational analysis allowed Delphine to reconsider the nature of the bonds between her different family members, as well as the context in which the secret was enacted. The broader outlook on the situation enabled her to make sense of life experiences she could not explain to herself so far. To restore a certain sense of balance I suggested that she break the silence and talk about the secret and share her views on it.

One day as she was visiting her mother, Delphine summoned the courage to speak out. Here is what she told me: "It was really difficult for me to speak to my mother—she's old now, she's not very well, and she's losing her memory. But she listened to me, and she said: 'I didn't know you felt that way.' I felt she was sincere. Ten days later, she called me and asked me to forgive her for all the suffering her silence had caused. I'll remember that day as full of sunshine. I told her that her reaching out to me would no doubt help me and other family members to heal. She replied: 'Yes, I also want to heal'."

To be able to talk with her mother about her secret opened to new integration perspectives. Delphine now knows she can rely on her partner, on the thawing of the relations in her family, and even on her older sister's children and grandchildren who appreciate the work she did to heal. Putting this unspoken family secret into words was the first most crucial step to assimilate the consequences of her mother's secret. Thanks to this, she became able to assimilate her past and protect succeeding generations from the consequences of this family secret. A year later she wrote to me, "by putting words on my pain and writing a letter about it, read by my whole family, I have now found a deep peace in the relationship with my mother."

Dealing with her mother's unfinished story

Another example demonstrates how unfinished conflicts can be transmitted across three generations of women. A mother came to consult me to better understand why she kept on reliving experiences similar to those of her grandmother. Since she was a child, Micheline had been constantly compared to her grandmother. The parallels between her life and her grandmother's were so uncanny that she and those around her could not help noticing them. Specifically, after they had each lost their husband, they both became mistresses to wealthy men who did not want to leave their depressive and medicated wives. When Micheline underwent screening for pancreatic cancer, she became afraid she might suffer the same fate as her grandmother, who had died from pancreatic cancer at the age of fifty-four. While the earlier resemblances surprised and amused her, the latter was a serious warning. She decided to seek help since she no longer felt in control of her destiny.

Micheline's transgenerational analysis allowed her to understand how the conflictual relationship between her mother and her grandmother, had been repeated by her mother in her relation to Micheline, and this was especially apparent in her feelings of abandonment. In hindsight, she remembered feeling even at a young age that it was her responsibility to help her mother. She felt so strongly that it was her mission to help her mother repair her relationship with her own mother that she had put her own needs aside.

Then one day, Micheline told me about a slip of the tongue her mother had made that really struck her. She repeated the words her mother had used when, in her father's presence, they were introduced to some acquaintances: 'And here is my daughter and her husband,' instead of saying, 'And here is my daughter and my husband.' To understand this slip, you need to know that for Micheline's mother, her husband had taken on the role of her own father, who had been deported to Siberia—a significant and traumatic episode that we had previously discussed. Her mother's slip of the tongue revealed that the person she was referring to wasn't Micheline, but her own mother, 'Here is my mother and her husband.' Indeed, if her husband represented her father, then her daughter represented her mother. This slip of the tongue exposed the transfer of the mother figure onto her daughter. This realization was liberating for Micheline, as it provided her with the key to understanding that her mother was placing her in the role of her grandmother.

To explain these types of situations, specialists in this field describe a process known as 'parentification.' When caught in their parents' emotional dynamics, a child may unconsciously align with these unspoken expectations, re-enacting the unresolved stories of their ancestors and unconsciously shaping their own future.

By clarifying her grandmother's past and the conflictual relationship between her grandmother and her mother, Micheline was progressively able to free herself from her role as her mother's helper. Such an awareness allowed her to view herself as an independent woman who did not need to carry the burden of what went wrong between her mother and grandmother. She learned to differentiate herself from her grandmother and better understand the troubling events that had impacted her life. Indeed, becoming her own Self allowed Micheline to rewrite unexplained parts of her story, relegating them to her history, and preventing them from spilling over into her present life.

Another example of transgenerational analysis will allow us to gain a better understanding of unconscious inheritances. Marc Wolynn describes the situation of Gretchen, a woman who suffered from depression and anxiety despite years of antidepressant medication and multiple group therapies. "Gretchen told me she no longer wanted to live. For as long as she could remember, she had struggled with emotions so intense she could barely contain the surges in her body. Gretchen had been admitted several times to a psychiatric hospital where she was diagnosed as bipolar with a severe anxiety disorder. Medication brought her slight relief but never touched the powerful suicidal urges that lived inside her. Her depression and anxiety, she said, had prevented her from ever marrying and having children. In a surprisingly matter-of-fact tone of voice, she told me that she was planning to commit suicide before her next birthday."[11] Marc Wolynn decided to dig deeper and ask how she planned to commit suicide. Gretchen said she wanted to evaporate. She planned to jump into a molten steel tank at a factory where her brother worked. "My body will incinerate in seconds," she said. Marc Wolynn had often heard words such as these from his patients who were descendants of victims of the Holocaust. As a result, he asked Gretchen if someone in her family was Jewish or had been involved in the Holocaust. After a moment of hesitation, Gretchen remembered her grandmother's story. Born into a Jewish family in Poland, her grandmother later converted to Catholicism when she moved to America and married Gretchen's grandfather in 1946. Two years earlier, her whole family had died in the gas chambers at Auschwitz. They were killed with toxic gas and then incinerated. This story was never passed down. No one ever talked of the war, nor of the family members who were incinerated. On the contrary, the events were trivialized.

For Marc Wolynn, it became clear that the symptoms Gretchen presented were rooted in her grandmother's tragic story. It seemed as if no one in the family had ever considered grieving all these ancestors who had died in such tragic circumstances. "As I explained the connection, Gretchen listened intently. Her eyes widened and color rose in her cheeks. I could tell that what I said was resonating. For the first time, Gretchen had an explanation for her suffering that made sense to her."

To help Gretchen assimilate her unconscious reality, Wolynn asked her to imagine how her grandmother might feel regarding the situation she had described. This exercise brought up difficult feelings of loss, pain, solitude

---

[11] Marc Wolynn (2016), *It didn't start with you*, Viking, New York.

and isolation, as well as strong feelings of guilt (which many descendants of victims of extermination feel). "When Gretchen was able to access these sensations, she realized that her wish to annihilate herself was deeply entwined with her lost family members. She also realized that she had taken on some element of her grandmother's desire to die. As Gretchen absorbed this understanding, seeing the family story in a new light, her body began to soften, as if something inside her that had long been coiled up could now relax."

Claude Nachin provides another example that shows how events that have not been properly integrated by one's ancestors can have an impact on their descendants. A woman consulted him on account of a phobia of the cold and frigidity issues[12]. One day, in contrast to her usual manner of speaking, she said that she had suicidal thoughts and mentioned that her aunt was depressed again. Upon deeper exploration, it appeared that neither her mother nor her aunts had grieved the loss of their father, who had been hydrocuted[13] while on vacation with his mistress (long before the birth of the patient). Her symptoms thus took on a new meaning: they unconsciously referred to a story that had not been integrated by her mother and her aunts. Her symptoms (precautions against the cold and sexual inhibition) were linked to the death of her grandfather. The unspeakable context surrounding it prevented the family from mourning. Indeed, her symptoms demonstrated that the death of her grandfather had not yet been integrated. It manifested itself through the difficulties the descendant faced. Once the significance of her symptoms was brought to light, she could start to assimilate them.

---

[12] Claude Nachin (2001), "Unité duelle, crypte et fantômes", in *La psychanalyse avec Nicolas Abraham et Maria Torok*, under the direction of Jean-Claude Rouchy, Éres, Paris, p. 47.

[13] Death provoked by immersion in freezing water.

These examples demonstrate the therapeutic potential of unveiling the unconscious heritage of unfinished family stories. They reveal the existence of a link between conflicts inherited from ancestors and current symptoms. Such associations, which characterize all approaches said to be "transgenerational," give the symptoms new meaning, and are an important step for transgenerational integration and healing.

The value of transgenerational integration is not limited to its therapeutic use. This work may also be viewed as a form of personal development. Becoming aware of one's unconscious loyalties is a way out of alienating heritages, a way to get closer to oneself.

In ancient times, the inheritor was regarded not just as a victim but also as someone through whom a family, or a unit of individuals, could heal from unfinished stories stemming back to their ancestors. Pierre Ramaut explains that "the ancient Chinese believed that a 'transgenerational mandate', originating from a person's connection to their ancestors, could be given, by fate to one of the last descendants of the lineage. This person is 'mandated' to heal the unfinished stories of the family tree and integrate them through their life path." [14]

Depth Psychology and the transgenerational unconscious

Although it is commonly believed that the transgenerational perspective implies that we should turn to the past, one must understand that it is not the past itself which affects the descendants, but rather its current unconscious consequences. These are even more present—here and now—as they have become unconscious. In therapy, this

---

[14] Pierre Ramaut (2016), « Transgenerational Psychoanalysis and Shamanism to Heal from Ghosts», in *Shamanism, Ancestors and Transgenerational Integration*, Genesis Editions, Geneva.

encompasses deciphering the unconscious meaning behind the symptoms. So, our attention primarily focuses on analysing the action of the unconscious in the present moment, and only symbolically to the unfinished stories of our ancestors.

The timelessness of the unconscious resonated with the discoveries of the Depth Psychology pioneers. They had previously explained how non-integrated problems could persist over time, like a debt waiting to be settled. Freud observed a tendency to repeatedly encounter the same issues, a phenomenon he called "repetition compulsion." This recurring pattern of problems seemed to reflect a need to bring unconscious memories to the surface. Towards the end of his life, Freud put his finger on what we recognize today as the transgenerational unconscious. "The archaic heritage of man is not only composed of predispositions but also of ideological contexts and traces of memory, left behind by the experiences of previous generations."[15] In this excerpt from his last book, Freud was planting a new seed for his readers to sow. Ironically, while defending Freudian dogmas against Jung's notion of the collective unconscious, Freud's supporters missed out on his last important perspectives.

For his part, Jung analyzed his genealogy and was able to determine the importance of the transgenerational for himself. "While working on my family tree, I understood how my destiny attached me to my ancestors. I very much feel that I am under the influence of things and problems that were left incomplete and unanswered by my parents, my grandparents, and my other ancestors. I have always thought that I, too, had to answer the same questions that destiny had already posed to my ancestors, and to which they had not found the answers, or that I had needed to

---

[15] Sigmund Freud, *Moses and Monotheism, three essays*, Hogarth Press, (1878), London, p.99.

resolve or simply carry forward challenges that previous generations left unfinished."[16] Although he had done a significant amount of transgenerational integration work, Jung did not theorize it as thoroughly as he could have. Nevertheless, his work contributed to the growing field of transgenerational analysis. For example, he explained that whatever does not emerge into conscious form will come back in the form of destiny.

Each in their own way, Freud, Jung, and other pioneers of Depth Psychology have put forward natural laws suggesting how the psyche functions and how to access its secrets. To analyze the transgenerational unconscious, these pioneers have left us the best tools possible: the analysis of transferences[17] and listening more intently to the unconscious and symbolic meaning behind symptoms.

While Depth Psychology established the link between repressed and denied experiences and unconscious contents, it had not gone beyond studying the unconscious and its link to early childhood. Since then, we have been able to recognize the impact of the intrauterine experience, allowing a more complete understanding of the bonds of filiation. Today, we know that our unconscious is also made up of the transgenerational legacies left to us by our ancestors. The debts we may contract during our own lives can repeat and amplify the ones we inherited from our forefathers. Famous in psychoanalytical literature, the "return of the repressed" (otherwise known as the awakening of the unconscious in the form of symptoms) is also tied to these transgenerational legacies.

The clarification of our genealogy helps to know what alienates us - our shadows. Transgenerational analysis facilitates access to these unconscious parts to know oneself

---

[16] Carl Jung (1966), *Memories, Dream, Reflections*, Vintage, NY.

[17] The definition and functioning of transferences will be developed in chapter four.

better and to distinguish our Self from these transgenerational heritages alienating us. As therapeutic experience demonstrates, family trees are an excellent source of information to shed light on the present.

Moreover, transgenerational analysis offers a relatively simple and effective way to start introspective work. Solutions are found within, replacing the need to project our unconscious conflicts onto the outside world. As will be discussed in another chapter, the lack of integration is at the origin of our projections. The transgenerational approach allows us to unveil the sources that shape our perception of reality. This type of analysis is timely, as it offers new perspectives for addressing the challenges of our hypermodern world, both on an individual and collective scale. This discipline offers an alternative approach to the classic "explanatory" therapy and overcomes the shortcomings of the medical model, as well as the all too general standards established by the DSM[18].

Early transgenerational analysis

Leopold Szondi (1893-1986), a Hungarian doctor and psychologist who lived in Switzerland, and was influenced by Freud and Binswanger, was a precursor of the analysis of hereditary factors. He created a new discipline: *fate analysis,* which studies the influence of hereditary dispositions in the choices and destiny of man. His *Psychology of Destiny* seeks to "unveil the patterns and the family figures transmitted in the hereditary lot of the person as regressive ancestral constraints that guide choices in love and friendship, choice of profession, the form of sickness and the kind of death, in short, the destiny of the individual."[19]

---

[18] DSM, a medical reference for doctors that determines which symptoms should be medicalized and which should not.

[19] Szondi Léopold (1972), *Introduction à l'analyse du destin*, vol. 1, éditions Nauwlaerts, Paris.

Szondi recounts the case of a worker who, in order to obtain the money necessary for his planned expatriation, killed the cashier of his factory. Captured and sentenced to life imprisonment, he was released after fifteen years for good behavior. Szondi explains "he then became a preacher, married, and led a model religious life. In his family, we found criminals as well as a certain number of pastors."

Having identified the importance of hereditary determinism, Szondi also recognized the function of integration that he attributed to the "pontifex-ego," which is close to my definition of the self in its individuation and healing properties. He also recognized the existence of a family unconscious. "Closely linked in its functioning to the personal and repressed unconscious of Freud and to the collective unconscious of Jung [...] While classic psychoanalysis works wonders with neuroses, it fails when treating specific kinds of trauma—as Freud himself admitted in 1937—wherever the disturbance of the instinctual life and the ego is not due to personal experience of trauma but has been inherited from an earlier generation. For this category of psychic disease, the psychology of destiny (or fate analysis) has had to search for new ways of healing; all of which are connected with the unconscious and particularly with the possibilities of hidden family stories. By this very fact, we can affirm that *the psychology of destiny constitutes the bridge between genetics and the psychology of the depths.*"

In the 1970s, Nicholas Abraham and Maria Torok, both benefitting from phenomenological[20] and psychoanalytic training, also veered towards the fertile domain of transgenerational analysis. Like Ferenczi and Szondi, they

---

[20] A branch of philosophy which focuses first and foremost the idea of being and being there (Dasein). It can evoke a sort of mindfulness but with, at its center, an authentic self who truly thinks.

are Hungarian of origin. Since their first works[21] published in 1978, impressive transgenerational therapeutic testimony has built up. However, as surprising as it may seem, the term "transgenerational" was for a long time misunderstood by most psychoanalysts. Other therapists and psychotherapists did not wait around for psychoanalysts to understand it before integrating this dimension of the unconscious into their theory. For example, after having participated in the seminar given by Nicolas Abraham, Anne Ancelin Schützenberger developed a more pragmatic analysis, known as the *Genosociogram*, a sort of family tree which depicts more psycho-affective information.

Meanwhile, and independently from each other, many therapists have deciphered the bonds between ancestors and their descendants. To name a few of the best-known: Bert Hellinger (*family constellations*), Ivan Boszormenyi-Nagy (*family loyalty*), Serge Lebovici (*transgenerational mandates*), Rene Kaes (*inherited trauma*) and Alberto Eiguer, analyzing the "tribute to the ancestors." So even if they are issued from different schools, therapists are increasingly incorporating transgenerational analysis into their practices.

Despite these important developments in private therapeutic practices, the analysis of the unconscious continues to trigger considerable resistance in academic circles, which are historically bound to promote rationalism. This resistance has been further reinforced by the positivist medical model, giving rise to an even wider gap between the psychological need to give meaning to our experiences, and the growing policy of medicalizing the psyche.

[21] Nicolas Abraham and Maria Torok, *The Shell and the Kernel*: Renewals of Psychoanalysis, 1994, University of Chicago Press.

The unspoken and the unthinkable

Working on integrating family stories relies on the symbolization of all that was unthought of in the family tree. Elaborating psychological perspectives and seeking out rational or irrational truths will progressively counterbalance the unfinished or unintegrated stories of our ancestors. If they are not integrated, these stories may duplicate, and similar consequences may recur. Experience has also shown that over the generations, unspoken issues can take on heavier, unthinkable forms, sometimes resulting in destructive behaviors or acting out.

To analyze this transmission, Serge Tisseron[22] proposed a model over three generations: whatever has not been integrated by the first generation becomes unthinkable for the next generation (which is deprived of specific repressed words), while the third generation may resort to acting out or other symptomatic behaviors. This view parallels that of Francoise Dolto, who believes that it takes three generations to produce a psychosis. In other words, an unspoken thought or a secret kept by the first generation can lead to neurotic tendencies in the second generation, and psychotic tendencies and acting out in the third.

Never-ending conflicts, such as those of Sicilian vendettas, show the power of transgenerational alienation. Shakespeare illustrates this very well in his famous play *Romeo and Juliet*. Here, the Capulets and the Montagues determine their children's tragic destiny by perpetuating century-old conflicts.

---

[22] Serge Tisseron (1995), *Le psychisme à l'épreuve des générations : clinique du fantôme*, Dunod, Paris.

2
Ancient Origins

Attention to the connections between generations dates back far in history. The authors of *Shamanism, Ancestors and Transgenerational Therapy*[23] demonstrate the diverse manners in which traditional societies have dealt with transgenerational heritages.

The worship of ancestors, for example, preserved the memory of family histories, which prevented the lack of transmission—unlike what happens in our modern societies. This way of remembering family histories limited the transmission of transgenerational alienation, also known as "ancestor's syndrome." This worship of ancestors, a part of many ancient traditions, sought to maintain harmony and to ensure a healthy balance within the world. As a famous Chinese proverb best sums it up, *to forget one's ancestors is to be a brook without a source, a tree without roots.*

Origins of transgenerational awareness

The practice of ancestor worship predated that of religions. Widely spread in Asia, Africa, and even Europe, it reflected a desire for global harmony, between the dead and the living, the invisible world and the visible one.

Across East and Southeast Asia, in China, Korea, Japan, and Vietnam, ancestor worship was a widespread practice. Connecting with one's ancestors was not only a way

---

[23] *Shamanism, Ancestors and Transgenerational Therapy,* Tony T. Gaillard, C. Michael Smith, Olivier Douville, Pierre Ramaut, Elisabeth Horowitz, Iona Miller, Myron Eshowsky, 2020, Genesis Editions, Geneva.

for personal rooting, but also a privilege not everybody could pretend to—unless they were invited to it and ready to be initiated. For example, when incorporated into Buddhism, the practice became associated with new rules. In China, only the King could celebrate his ancestors going back seven generations. Princes could not go past the fifth generation, grand officers the third, and lay people just the first generation. The emperor, on the other hand, the "Son of Heaven", had to honour both Earth and Heaven, his symbolic "parents."

In Vietnam, ancestor worship also included the concept of transmission. The youngest would learn moral principles from their ancestors, how to love their work, and how to gather the courage to overcome difficulties. In addition, they were expected to pass on these life lessons to their own descendants.

In Japan, an altar was built in the holiest part of each home, with tablets bearing the names of their ancestors. During birthday ceremonies—still practiced today—ancestors were remembered and honoured with various rituals such as offerings of incense, sweetmeats, tea, and sutras chanting.

Even today, in dojos, meditation and yoga centers, you can find altars with pictures of the school's founder and their first students. As it was natural at the time, today's students would be wise to clarify their transgenerational legacies before engaging in such ancestral practices.

By cultivating their relationship with their ancestors, all were able to reconnect with their roots. Similarly, transgenerational integration prompts us to be active towards our transgenerational legacies rather than passively enduring them. Thus, as Goethe best puts it, "That which has been passed to you by inheritance from your ancestors, acquire it so that you may possess it." In other words, to avoid being possessed by an unconscious heritage, integrate it! In a similar perspective, the psychotherapist

Vincent de Gauléjac stated, “The individual is the product of a history from which they seek to become the subject.”

From a perspective of personal development, "bringing one's ancestors to life within oneself becomes a practice for oneself." This practice, especially in shamanism, extends to animals, plants, and minerals, in an attempt to live in harmony with all of creation. Initiations and rituals support this work of integration, leading to the guarantee of a happy and prosperous life, one which all traditions have always tried to protect.[24]

Let us not cut ourselves off from our roots

In these traditions, it is important to nurture above all else the timeless relation to one’s origins and to life itself. This is not accomplished by looking back towards the past, but rather, by integrating it in a way that allows the ancestors and the origins to remain symbolically alive in the present day. Jung[25] refers to the ancient Chinese “house of the ancestor” to explain that in that culture, “the central point of a human personality is the place where one’s ancestors are reincarnated.” This intimate relationship with ancestors and origins is the key to genuine personal fulfilment.

These ancient traditions teach us an essential first lesson: to become an individual, rather than cutting ourselves off from our parents or our roots, we should integrate them. This means managing our relationship with the problematic parts of our family tree to transform these unconscious inheritances into symbolic links with our family tree, down to our origins. Archetypes such as Mother Earth and the Celestial Father provide precisely this kind of symbolic way of relating to origins.

---

24 See Tony T. Gaillard & al. (2020), *Shamanism, Ancestors and Transgenerational Therapy*, Genesis Editions, Geneva.

25 Carl G. Jung, *Dream Analysis, Notes of the Seminar Given in 1928-30*, Routledge (1984).

This precept, not to cut oneself from where we come from, deserves to be considered in a contemporary approach to transgenerational therapy. For what becomes of a tree cut off from its roots? It is better to clarify and integrate the unthinkable in our genealogy rather than to try to cut it off—a fantasy typical of our modern culture. It is precisely to respect the link to our origins that I speak of transgenerational integration, a task for the Self, and not transgenerational "liberation," which would imply breaking deeply rooted bonds.

The Genealogy of Greek Gods

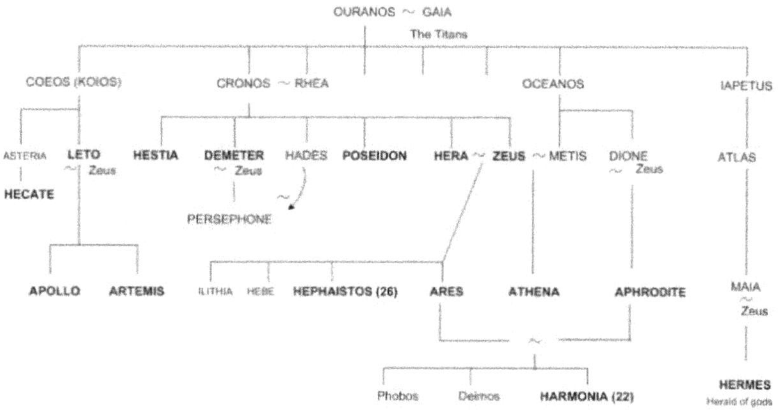

People had access to the first symbolic genealogy of their origins thanks to their founding myths and the work of Hesiod on the birth of the gods provided by their poets. This served as a model for their own family trees and to anchor them in the dawn of time. This connection to one's origins was of great importance. For instance, Hecataeus of Miletus claimed that by tracing back sixteen generations, he could claim descent from a god.

Testimonies of the awareness of transgenerational heritage can be found in mythology and between the lines of ancient stories. In the penultimate chapter, I will show that Sophocles' Oedipus myth illustrates a perfect mastery of transgenerational laws. He tells us about the consequences of hidden heritage, from Cadmus, the founder of Thebes, to Antigone.

Written traces

The awareness of transgenerational links can also be found in passages from ancient texts. These references are not theoretical like the ones we have today, they are metaphorical, mythological, and symbolic. For example, in the Bible we find statements like: "No branch can bear fruit by itself; it must remain in the vine"[26]

Transgenerational heritages have been represented in various ways, such as spirits that haunt the living. In the Bible, they are represented as curses based on an ancestor's sins, impacting several generations. Didier Dumas[27] pointed to such references to the sins of ancestors and their consequences in the Old Testament: "for I, the Lord your God, am a jealous God, punishing the children for the sins of the parents to the third and fourth generation of those who hate me, but showing love to a thousand generations of those who love me and keep my commandments."[28] Marie Balmary also cites the Bible. "The fathers eat sour grapes, and the children's teeth are set on edge"[29]. In the book of Job (8.8-9) we can also find, "Ask the former generations and find out what their fathers learned, for we were born only yesterday and know nothing."

Transgenerational links in ancient Greece

Transgenerational transmissions also resonated with the Ancient Greeks, who had assimilated many forms of knowledge from the Mediterranean Basin and the Middle East. To account for these transmissions, they often

---

[26] John, 15: 1-17.

[27] Didier Dumas (2001), *La Bible et ses fantômes*, de Brouwer, Paris.

[28] Exodus, XX, 2-6

[29] *Ezekiel* 18, 2 ff.; *Jeremiah* 31, 29.

evoked the *Ate*, an unwritten or divine law that connects the descendants to their ancestors through their blood ties as if they formed a single entity. It is important to remember that at that time, the notion of individuality did not exist the way we consider it today.

An excerpt from *The Iliad*[30] bears witness to the importance of the alliances forged by one's ancestors. During the Trojan War, Glaucus meets Diomedes, a Greek enemy. Each of them declares his genealogy, and the two men discover that at one time, Diomedes's grandfather Oenus, offered his hospitality to Glaucus's grandfather, Bellerophon. Bound by the ties of these good relations shared by their respective grandfathers, Glaucus and Diomedes choose not to fight each other, but instead exchange their arms as a sign of mutual respect. This anecdote demonstrates how strong respect for transgenerational bonds can outweigh other issues.

During Ancient Greek times, transgenerational heritages were governed by the *Ate*, a law to which they attributed the will of the Gods, and which today we consider to be an unconscious transgenerational phenomenon. For example, Eric Dodds reported that people who were not guilty, or not responsible, could nonetheless be hereditary victims of the faults committed by their ancestors. "Theognis complains that a system is unfair if it allows a criminal to escape while another is punished later. This can be unfair, but it seemed to be a law of nature that one had to accept. The family was a moral unit, the life of a son was the prolongation of the father, and the son inherited his father's moral and commercial debts. Eventually, the debt must be paid. As Pythia had told Croesus, the causal link between crime and punishment was *moira*, something that not even a God could break. Croesus had to endure the

[30] Homer, *The Iliad*, Book VI, v.119 ff.

consequences of whatever crime had been committed by an ancestor, five generations before him".[31]

A prevalent idea during Ancient Greek times was that of divine justice. Even if it were not exercised immediately, it would be eventually, and "it could be said that the unpunished sinner suffered through his descendants, or that he would pay his debt in person in another life." Gustave Glotz also insisted on these transgenerational links in Antiquity. "Whether man likes it or not, punishment is handed down from father to son, because this is the will of the Gods. It is a law of nature. Even those who consider it immoral admit that it exists."[32]

Therefore, even though knowledge was primarily transmitted orally during this era, there exist enough written records to demonstrate how omnipresent the transgenerational was in the collective consciousness in that time. Such references allow us to believe that transgenerational integration cannot be reduced to a momentary trend in the therapeutic field. Rather, these ancient references show us that we need to revive this almost forgotten knowledge.

Reconnection with our origins

From a traditional perspective, the family line looks like a root system that connects us to our origins, symbolized in mythology by divine and totemic figures. Indeed, the worshipping of ancestors goes as far as idolizing some of them or making them intercessors with the Gods. Increasingly symbolic, this relationship with the origins transcends temporal history, towards a timeless dimension that embraces the past, the present, and the future all at once.

---

[31] Eric R. Dodds (1951), *The Greeks and the Irrational,* University of California Press.

[32] Gustave Glotz (1904), *La solidarité dans la famille grecque*, Albert Fontemoing, Paris, p. 575.

We can now understand that the rituals and spiritual practices of the time were not so much about maintaining a faltering faith, but about experiencing and celebrating the living, and loving, experience of a relationship with the origins. In other words, the religious practices of the time (not always comparable with the practices of today) fulfilled a function of communion with one's origins, both symbolic and spiritual.

Today, we understand that this traditional knowledge nurtured a healthy relationship with our origins, thus preventing "ancestor syndrome" from occurring. The reason for taking care of one's genealogy is therefore to maintain this original connection, the alliance with the forces of life, and experiencing one's lively true Self.

These ancient wisdoms offer another lesson for our understanding of transgenerational dynamics. A parent who guides a child to become a true subject is remembered as an ancestor and an inspiration. This role ensures that the parent enters history and will not be forgotten. For instance, the founder of Thebes, Cadmos, earns the right to enter the *Champs Élysées* as the father of all Thebans. The remembrance or worship of such a positive ancestor helps ensure the prosperity of future generations. As we shall see, in his testamentary work *Oedipus at Colonus*, Sophocles highlights the importance of preserving the memory of Oedipus to guarantee the prosperity.

Therefore, beyond family ties, ancient teaching emphasizes reconnecting with one's origins and honoring good ancestors—those who helped their children to develop as true selves while preventing them from inheriting unfinished stories. This second lesson is less about historical accuracy and more about a timeless, symbolic, and functional dimension. Similar to rites of passage, a person becomes a member of the adult community after assimilating their symbolic origins. These origins then continue to live within the person, allowing their individualization.

Depending on the tradition, different divine figures represent symbolic parents, often associated with Heaven and Earth. A symbolic parental function is delegated to this original couple; they guarantee the balance of the world. As the philosopher Michel Serres explains, "We are not simply a creation of our parents, but the result of thousands of years of evolution." We are part of a story that began long before our parents, who only perpetuate it, without necessarily adding new elements to it. A passage in the *Corpus Hermeticum* clarifies this relationship with the origins: "Who then created all these things? What mother, what father, but the invisible God who, by his own will, made everything? No one says that a statue or a painting could have been created without a sculptor, or a painter, so could this Creation have come to be without a Creator? [...] Never, O my son Tat, separate the works created from their Creator". The hermetic tradition even goes as far as to state that "no one in the Universe exists without a mother or a father."[33]

In this perspective, the parental role is to initiate their children until they integrate this symbolic relation to their origins. It is this connection that then takes over the parental support. Even in a religious form, learning such a symbolic language can establish a constructive dialogue with one's origins, where the mind (or soul) can be nourished and healed—just as the ancients explained.

In order not to break with this ancient wisdom, contemporary therapy should also consider the integration of our symbolic origins, whether they be scientific (BigBang), religious (the story of man's origin), or mythological (Theogony). As I propose, *transgenerational integration* seeks to do so and prefers to recognize and support a desire to be more rooted, as opposed to encouraging the

---

[33] Hermès Trismégiste (2011), *Corpus Hermeticum*, Tome I, les Belles Lettres, Paris, p. 63.

illusion of freedom by trying to cut oneself loose from one's roots. This modern belief that one could gain from being cut from its unconscious heritage is a superficial defense mechanism. It only makes things worse while unconscious debt increases, generating all kinds of symptoms, such as environmental debt on a collective scale.

Beyond cultural differences

The transformation of civilization that took place in Athens, the rationalization of the world (which some authors refer to as the disenchantment of the world), resulted in the gradual loss of transgenerational consciousness. While it remains important to shed light on familial events that cause their transmission to be altered, one must also be aware of the reasons that have led our modern society to forget about transgenerational laws.

Understanding what has been lost from such a change of civilization, sheds light on the forces, that even today, repress the transgenerational consciousness. These forces are omnipresent in a culture that is partly founded on such repression. However, despite such resistance, there exists a growing interest in reviving ancient wisdom. The number of domains referring to traditional knowledge is constantly growing. We can see it in health, lifestyle, nutrition, yoga, agriculture, permaculture, and new economic models concerned with the ecological footprint. These different domains all go against the tide of our hypermodern culture and its founding repressions.

Transgenerational integration refers to ancient wisdom we can associate with contemporary forms of therapy. Beyond the benefit of better understanding one's family history, what better way to reappropriate an almost forgotten legacy than with transgenerational analysis? Based on this ancient knowledge, the relationship with our origins should be recognized as a path to meet our inalienable part, which I call the Self.

3
The Transgenerational Unconscious

Transgenerational patterns show up through repeated behaviors and the defense mechanisms they trigger, sometimes leading to visible symptoms. The latter call for our attention, prompting us to consider the unconscious parts that inhabit us.

When we begin to address unresolved histories, we must avoid relying on simplistic explanations. Indeed, our unconscious and emotional conditioning often makes us react just as our ancestors did, which risks perpetuating the same unresolved issues and reinforcing old conflicts. Among these reactions, using explanations is very common. But explaining something is not the same as understanding or integrating it. Only true integration allows us to find peace.

Furthermore, when analyzing the lives of our ancestors, we must remember that in the face of "inhumane" situations, people often fail to engage in healthy psychological processing. In extreme circumstances, they are more likely to resort to primitive defense mechanisms such as denial, splitting, and repression.

Because they operate in unconscious ways, it is difficult to ascertain the influence transgenerational legacies have on our lives. However, by being more attentive, anyone can observe examples of transgenerational transmission. Young mothers who had vowed not to replicate their mothers' actions often find themselves, though reluctantly, admitting that they have done just that. Similarly, fathers might end up repeating the same injunctions they once received as children, almost as if they have become replicas of their own parents.

Talking to Children

To avoid perpetuating the lack of integration, Francoise Dolto emphasizes the importance of not hiding significant events concerning adults, such as family deaths or extramarital paternity, from children. Not only do children possess a form of intuitive knowledge of these events, but more importantly, such duplicity provokes a compulsive need to find tangible explanations for the way they are feeling. This need may never be satisfied and consequently alienate their future. For example, we can draw parallels between teenagers who abuse drugs and alcohol, and parents who have "fixed" and repressed their problems by turning to drugs or medication themselves.

When asked what constitutes an error in terms of being responsible for transgenerational transmissions, Didier Dumas[34] explains, "An error? It's the absence of speech, an inability to speak, to assume oneself as a human being, a being of language." Psychoanalysts have long emphasized the crucial role that adult speech plays in the positive development of children. According to this perspective, the way adults communicate helps the child develop a true sense of self—an autonomous being capable of independent thought. The distinction between the purely biological role of parents and their role in fostering the development of the child's self is rooted in the concept of symbolic transmission, or, conversely, its absence.

---

[34] Nina Canault (1998), *Comment paye-t-on les fautes de ses ancêtres*, Desclée de Brouwer, Paris.

Inheriting secrets

Secrets, lies and the unspoken can have profound consequences for those who inherit them. Parents and grandparents who were unwilling or unable to acknowledge and speak about their difficulties may unconsciously pass these challenges on to their descendants. Secrets about one's father's identity, often the result of an extramarital affair, or in some cases, of secret adoptions (as in the case of Oedipus), are not without consequences.

In her book, Virginie Tyou[35] discusses how her secret filiation manifested itself through severe symptoms, which could only be healed after she had discovered the truth. By depriving children of a verbal transmission, allowing them to better cope with their lives, the unspoken has a dark and insidious influence on the individual, sometimes impacting several generations.

Jack Nicholson's life was marked by a secret about the identity of his mother, who pretended to be his sister. Elisabeth Horowitz analyzes the consequences of this lack of transparency, as well as the surprising coincidences regarding the roles he played in certain films. "The movie *Chinatown*, which has as its theme an incestuous secret, features a scene in which Faye Dunaway tells Nicholson about her child. 'I'm his mother, I'm his sister. I'm his mother and I'm his sister.' This scene was so close to Jack's own personal 'mother-sister' revelation, that many people wondered if Robert Towne, the scriptwriter and a friend of Nicholson, had a crystal ball and the ability to guess the untold truth." All the communication in the family was distorted by the secret. "The feeling of guilt is the inevitable corollary of the family strategy. How can one not feel guilty towards other family members after having cheated them for years? The position is perfectly untenable. Pro-

[35] Virginie Tyou (2016), *Voyage en mer intérieure*, Ker éditions.

tecting the parent by jealously guarding the secret (although its revelation would be essential to Nicholson's healthy development), is extremely distressing. Any meeting between those concerned will necessarily be tense and lacking in spontaneity."[36]

Elizabeth Horowitz finds another incident demonstrating the collateral effects of the secret. "John Nicholson, Jack's maternal grandfather (who had pretended to be his father), turned to drinking after being forced to be complicit in his wife's secret. He died prematurely at the age of 55. Murray, his father-in-law (who claimed to be his brother-in-law) also died prematurely of alcohol addiction. June, his mother who posed as his older sister, died prematurely of cancer at age 45, without ever revealing her secret. His half-brothers and sisters were also victims of the secret and grew up sincerely believing that Jack was their uncle. His Uncle Shorty and Aunt Lorraine needed to be seen as his brother-in-law and his sister respectively. Meanwhile, Jack's real father (Don Furcillo) was excluded entirely, and Jack knew none of his ancestors on his father's side. If Don Furcillo really is his father, then he is of Italian descent and not Irish as he had always been led to believe."

Inheriting collective non-integrated stories

Pascal Hachet, analyzing the history of the famous German drug addict and writer Christiane F. (Christiane Felscherinow), emphasizes her rejection of her parents and an entire generation that failed to integrate or discuss the psychological impact that World War II had on them. "This teenager's drug addiction will have been the expression of a ritual rejection of the influence of family secrets: to free the psyche of tensions that were as unbearable as

---

[36] Elisabeth Horowitz (2020), « Les secrets de famille de Jack Nicholson », in *Analyses transgénérationnelles pour mieux comprendre*, ouvrage collectif, tome 1, Genesis Editions, Geneva.

they were incomprehensible."[37] The way her ancestors hid their traumas led Christian F. to repeat them as if commanded to do so, which is typical of this kind of transgenerational alienation.

Among events that can lead to a lack of integration, wars, and genocide are of course major causes of transmitting trauma. While the heirs of incomplete mourning are not uncommon amongst the descendants of war victims, Peter Sichrovsky also observed traces of such trauma in the children and grandchildren of the oppressors, who carried with them heavy unconscious baggage. As the son of a German officer explains, "You know, the error is pursuing me. And the guilty one always ends up being punished. If it's not here and now, it will be at another moment, in another place. But it will eventually catch up with me. I cannot escape it. You will hear nothing from me, nothing, not even a word. What they did will remain a secret. No one may know it. Their actions, or rather their abuses, may never be talked about. My parents are burning in hell. They have been dead for a long time; for them, it is over. But I'm still here. Born guilty, sentenced to live a guilty life. The dreams, that's the worst part. They constantly haunt me at night. It's always the same dream. I know it as well as a movie I have seen a hundred times. They pull me out of bed, drag me out of my room and down the stairs, and push me into a car. Men in striped uniforms. The car drives through the city. I hear noises coming from outside. Some people shout 'Hurrah!', scream, and howl. I have trouble breathing, there's a knot in my throat. I rush to the door and try to open it. I shake it, I shout out, my eyes are burning; then, I wake up."[38]

---

[37] Pascal Hachet (2001) « Traumas collectifs, mythes, rites et toxicomanie », dans *La psychanalyse avec Nicolas Abraham et Maria Torok*, edited by Rouchy J.-C., Erès, Ramonville Ste Anne.

[38] Peter Sichrovsky (1989), *Born Guilty: Children of Nazi Families*, Basic Books, NY.

In one of her books, Anne-Ancelin Schützenberger describes the story of a family traumatized by the Armenian genocide of April 24, 1915. A woman had been shocked to discover the severed heads of her sisters and mother. Three generations later, two sisters gave birth to children with serious cerebral problems. "One must admit that it comes as a shock to discover that all these women were hairdressers. The grandmother saw heads cut off; ever since, all the daughters have been involved in fixing and embellishing heads, except for one who is an anesthesiologist/resuscitator—perhaps she is repairing death?"[39]

Such repetitions are also found in connection with geographical places. Myron Eshowsky[40] provides the example of Kosovo, an area in the Balkans where conflict flared up following the dissolution of Yugoslavia. "This region was where the First World War had begun, as well as the site of the war between the Ottomans (Muslim Turks) and the Serbs (Orthodox Christians) for supremacy in the Balkans during the Middle Ages. The battle of Kosovo ended in 1389 with the defeat of the Serbs by the Ottomans. And it was on the anniversary of this defeat that Archduke Ferdinand was killed by a Serbian militant, to avenge the humiliation of Serbia. This changed the entire European geopolitical situation. And, surprisingly enough, it was on this same date that Slobodan Milosevic, President of Serbia, made a call to arms during the Balkan Wars and invoked the battle of Kosovo: "No more will Islam enslave the Serbs."

---

39 Anne-Ancelin Schützenberger (1998), The Ancestor Syndrome: Transgenerational Psychotherapy and the Hidden Links in the Family Tree, Routledge, London, p. 72.

40 Myron Eshowsky (2020), « History that Never Ends: Healing Transgenerational Trauma in Community », in *Shamanism, Ancestors and Transgenerational Integration*, Genesis Editions.

Alienating loyalty

According to what Ivan Boszormenyi-Nagy[41] calls "unconscious family loyalty," children sometimes absorb difficulties like a sponge. This happens because these issues are neither discussed openly nor humanized, and the true nature of the problems is not communicated or addressed honestly. Events that are not psychologically integrated, that are not talked about, and cannot be mentioned without denial or discomfort, generate a pathogenic weight that can potentially be alienating. Serge Tisseron explains that a child can be exposed to "seepage of a secret" and mixed messages. For instance, the mention of a particular word or image might make a father tense up, causing him to distance himself from his child because it triggers an unpleasant memory. As we shall see, exposure to such non-verbal messages generates all kinds of symptomatic reactions, such as the development (from childhood) of the "false self" or "persona", or a narcissistic personality.

At the family level, conflicts can engender compensation mechanisms that are transmitted to the descendants, conditioning them, without allowing a proper integration of the past. Guy Ausloos[42] mentions the case of a young Englishman who paid heavily for his unconscious family heritage. He remained in Africa during the struggle for independence, while all his compatriots went home to England. He stayed because he felt the need to live up to his family motto, "Face up to it!" This caused him a lot of problems and a serious disability. Later, doing some research, he discovered that his family history had provoked this situation. One of his ancestors, the admiral of the British fleet, had chosen to save his ships and crews

---

[41] Ivan Boszormenyi-Nagy, (1980), *Psychothérapies familiales*, PUF, Paris.

[42] Guy Ausloos (1980), "Œdipe et sa famille, ou les secrets sont faits pour être agis", in *Dialogue*, n°70, AFCCC, Paris.

when he thought he was going to be defeated by the French. The government accused him of being a traitor and banished him. Cast out from the English gentry, the family reacted by changing its name and adopting a new motto, "Face up to it," to atone for the shame and erase the memory of this ancestor. The motto harmed the young Englishman, who was incapable of recognizing the danger of remaining in Africa.

Becoming aware of such unconscious loyalty to our ancestor's bypass can facilitate transgenerational integration, as in the case of Ingrid. This young, lively, independent woman had requested a consultation because she felt lost, caught up in a situation that made her unhappy. She had reconnected with a married man, despite having broken up with him several years ago. Her feelings were so strong that she felt completely lost. She saw no future. This situation affected both her personal and professional life.

By exploring the life of her ancestors, we discovered that her great-grandfather had rejected his wife after she had borne him a son. At that time, in North Africa, men held all the rights and polygamy was widespread. Ingrid confessed that she had always felt ambivalent towards polygamy and polyandry as if they were commonplace. It should be noted that as a child, she knew that her father had mistresses and had sided with him because her mother was highly dependent and seemed to settle into the role of victim. It is therefore no wonder that Ingrid could imagine herself happier as a mistress than as a wife. At that time, however, she questioned everything. The forced separation of her great-grandmother from her son had come to light, and this had repercussions for the boy and his descendants, including her father. Now, Ingrid saw things differently. I suggested that in this type of patriarchal tradition, the men are also victims of their unconscious loyalty towards their ancestors and that they had not integrated their inheritances either. Both men and women need to confront their transgenerational legacies to assimilate them. Ingrid's reaction was immediate; it was as though she had awakened. She shared that she had come to see herself differently and realized that, deep down, she did not align with the polygamous traditions of her ancestors. From that moment on, she decided to stop playing a passive role in her romantic relationship. Until then, her unconscious and limiting loyalty had prevented her from demanding more from the man she loved, despite the circumstances. She now listens to her inside voice which speaks of her desires, her need for recognition, and to have a more engaged partner in her life. To put it simply, by gaining awareness of her transgenerational loyalty, she was able to move beyond the role of a mistress and connect with her own needs.

Without awareness of alienating transgenerational loyalties, it is not uncommon to see descendants of ancestors affected by ethnic racism, sexual abuse, slavery, and other forms of trauma who, instead of engaging in integrative healing, focus on their ancestor's grievances and become even more alienated Therefore, instead of pacifying the past and the present, and distinguishing their lives from those of their ancestors, they tend to lose themselves in the conflictual heritage, potentially aggravating the situation.

Therapeutic experience also indicates that unintegrated events recur on specific dates. It is as if an unconscious memory that associates an experience with a particular time, imposes a repetition of the old history. Anne-Ancelin Schützenberger speaks of an "anniversary syndrome" whenever events are re-enacted on the same date or in similar circumstances.

For example, she recounts the story of a young doctor, 27 years old, who had a minor car accident while driving his six-year-old son to school for the first time. Anne-Ancelin Schützenberger suggested he investigate whether similar events had occurred in his family's history. Indeed, it turned out that "when he was six years old, on the way to school for the first time with his father, they had a car accident on October 1st. His father had experienced a similar accident as a child when going to school for the first time with his own father (the grandfather). The grandfather had not been in a similar accident as a child because he never went to school. His father had just been killed at the battle of Verdun. Because his family was very poor the boy had to tend to the cows and missed school. Ever since, at the beginning of each school year, in every generation, there had been a car accident on the way to school."[43]

Incomplete mourning

Sometimes to avoid dealing with the grief of a child, parents will create, more or less consciously, a *replacement child*. The latter will inherit the weight of this incomplete bereavement, and sometimes even the name of the child who has passed away. By not dealing effectively with such an event, archaic defense mechanisms (such as denial, repression, etc.) are triggered, repressing the memory of these events which then become unconscious and thus, endlessly present.

Children born on the same day as a deceased sibling may also become 'replacement children,' potentially experiencing alienation due to the unresolved grief. As Salomon Sellam has shown, in some cases, these replacement children are even conceived on the anniversary of the sibling's death. Therefore, we should also consider the date nine months prior to the child's birth to determine if they

[43] Anne-Ancelin Schützenberger (1998), *The Ancestor Syndrome: Transgenerational Psychotherapy and the Hidden Links in the Family Tree*, Routledge, London.

are the heir to an unmourned family member or a "ghost." Salomon Sellam tells the story of a young woman who complained about the sad, taciturn behavior of her son, Roman, otherwise in perfect health. We learned that this woman had had two miscarriages of two infants whose names would have been Romain and Anne. The name she gave her son was associated with both foetuses such that he ended up carrying the burden of the two incomplete griefs. "After a moment of reflection, marked by a pained expression and a few tears, she finally understood the simple truth: little Roman was burdened with the weight of Romain and Anne. The loss of these two children had never been truly mourned, and Roman carried the memory of these miscarriages. He could never fully enjoy life like a typical child, as he was expected to somehow make up for the loss of the two children in his parents' eyes."[44] This is how parents may unconsciously pass on their own lack of integration to the new generations.

Nicolas Abraham illustrates how incomplete mourning can be passed down to future generations. To understand the underlying causes of his client's great discomforts, Abraham suggested that the client delve into the lives of his ancestors. In doing so, the client realized that no one had ever spoken to him about his maternal grandfather. He discovered that the latter had been accused of bank robbery and had likely committed other worse crimes. Sent to the "Africa battalions, to break rocks," he was ultimately executed in a gas chamber. This discovery was significant for the client who was an amateur geologist. On weekends, he went out breaking rocks and hunted and collected large butterflies that he killed in a jar of cyanide. There was a clear and important connection between his activities as a geologist, as a butterfly collector,

---

[44] Salomon Sellam, *Exemples d'intégration transgénérationnelle*, collective book (2020, Genesis Editions), and *Le syndrome du gisant*, (2007, Bérangel), Saint-André-de-Sagonis.

and his grandfather's life. Because the latter was kept a secret, the client had inherited his grandfather's story, which he was unconsciously echoing in his hobbies. These seemingly innocent activities revealed the presence of "another" deep inside of him—his grandfather, who had never been discussed. This situation highlights a form of alienation: the presence of another within the descendant who, through his actions, evokes the unintegrated story of his family. By uncovering this secret, it was possible for the client to better understand the lack of integration he had inherited from his mother—and restoring a dialogue with life

André, a teacher at a social work school, had begun a course to become a psychotherapist. He told me he was interested in analyzing his family history, particularly because his grandfather had died young in a bike accident, and his father had also died young in a traffic accident. André described his father as experiencing intense outbursts of violence that sometimes seemed delusional. But fortunately, he had been a policeman and thus on the good side of the law. Yet, when André's paternal grandmother passed away, his father's distress escalated dangerously. In his anguish, he threatened to use his rifle on those around him. But André was able to stay calm and intervene to prevent harm. This incident underscored how profoundly the family struggled with processing loss and grief.

Following the divorce of his parents when he was two, André was entrusted to his paternal grandmother, who lived in a family countryside inn. He shared a bed with her, and since his paternal grandfather was also named André, he found himself becoming a representation of his grandfather in his grandmother's eyes.

For several months, André underwent a "classic" analytical psychotherapy, using a couch. He was pleased to see positive changes in his professional and private life.

Matters took a turn when the story surrounding his great-grandparents who had bought the inn was clarified. From the beginning of his therapy, the enigma of why he seemed to symbolically replace his deceased grandfather in his grandmother's bed persisted. New information helped to integrate the invisible strands of that history. André learned that before coming to live in this inn, his great-grandfather had lost his first wife and had remarried in 1900. Perhaps because he did not properly mourn the loss of his first wife, or for other unknown reasons, the new couple had three stillborn children. It was only when they changed their lives, and moved to the inn, that they had healthy children, including André's grandmother born in 1908. However, there were other deaths such as that of his grandmother's sister, who died accidentally at age fourteen, and one of her half-brothers who died at war in 1914.

Both his great-grandparents and grandmother had a long list of prematurely deceased loved ones, as if the incomplete mourning of the first of them had led to further difficult or impossible grieving. Indeed, his grandmother had also lost her husband when he was only thirty-seven years old. During therapy, all the ghosts haunting his grandmother's psyche were brought out into the open, identified, recognized, and placed back into the family history. Sharing his grandmother's bed had exposed him to all these unspoken stories. While integrating all these elements, André went to visit the family cemetery to appease himself and his family towards the memory of his ancestors.

By clarifying these unspoken stories with his family, two "therapeutic" consequences emerged. André better understood what alienated his grandmother and why she sometimes turned to alcohol. He also made more sense of his father's fits of violence, which expressed both his father's and the family's incomplete mourning. As expected,

André's relationship to his father changed. André could from then on appreciate and be proud of some of his father's qualities such as his natural authority. The second benefit was that this clarification fostered a renewed sense of connection to his ancestors and origins. For André, this link sometimes appeared to him as synchronicities, and a more inspired and poetic relationship to life.

This example illustrates well the secondary benefits that can be derived from a better understanding of our ancestors' unfinished stories. Beyond addressing a client's therapeutic needs, transgenerational integration also allows individuals to restore their connection to their origins. As discussed in the last chapter, a perfect model of that kind of transformation was left to us by Sophocles' Oedipus, who, by integrating his transgenerational legacies, ultimately becomes the benefactor of his hosts, ensuring the lasting prosperity of Colonus.

4
Transferences Between Generations

In this chapter, we will examine how unfinished stories are passed down through generations. More specifically, we will analyze the role of transference in transgenerational transmission, a well-known process in Depth Psychology.

Transferential needs

Transference is a spontaneous tendency to project unintegrated past experiences onto present-day situations. For example, a person who has been disappointed in love and who has not properly integrated this event will tend to project the prospect of renewed disappointment onto a new relationship.

Unfinished stories are at the origin of what I call a "transferential need." *Transferential needs* are bound to unintegrated life events which will be projected onto different aspects of the present moment. They are responsible for the repetition of these unfinished stories. To avoid a vicious cycle of repetition and prevent the stories from being reinforced, they require more awareness, and more presence when they recur. This is where the therapist's contribution can make a difference.

Selma Fraiberg provides us with a good example of transference. A young mother could no longer abide the tyranny of her 11-month-old son. She felt he was a "monster" who threw terrible temper tantrums and never gave her a moment's peace. She could not even go to the toilet without him bothering her. “He wants everything I have... if I am eating, he wants my bread, my coffee, my orange juice... he always ends up getting what he wants... he is deliberately trying to drive me out of my mind.” [45]

When the young mother was encouraged to talk about herself, it finally came out that the “real” monster had originated from her childhood. She had unconsciously kept the memory of her older brother. He was brutal and tyrannical, driving her to lock herself in her room and to weep with despair. To complete the picture that she projected onto her son; her brother was also her mother’s favorite. Gradually, she became aware of the relationship between the monster she saw reflected in her child, and the non-integrated history from her childhood. Under other circumstances, it wouldn’t be unrealistic to imagine that a child burdened by his mother’s projections might eventually embody[46] them. Such a child, adapting himself to the transferential needs of his mother, would be alienated by that “other” who haunted his mother’s unconscious mind—here her brother. By taking on the transference of his mother, the child would inherit her failure to integrate her experience and be alienated by it. However, thanks to the therapist’s input, the young mother was able to address the origin of her transferential needs rather than perpetuating them.

This kind of transferential need explains one part of transgenerational transmission, which lies upstream, as a result of non-integrated events. This is where transgenerational heritages are coming from, to be distinguished from a pole, downstream, that would be a receiver—and that we will analyze in the next chapter.

---

[45] Selma Fraiberg (1999), *Fantômes dans la chambre d’enfants*, PUF, Paris, p.109.

[46] We know that human beings have this faculty to adapt, even at their own expense, to justify the most unusual situations.

What is transference?

A pioneer in Depth Psychology, Sándor Ferenczi observes that "this tendency in neurotic people to engage in transference does not only manifest itself in the context of psychoanalytic cure, nor solely in relationship to a doctor. In fact, transference appears to be a mechanism of the psyche, which is a basic characteristic of neurosis in general, manifesting itself in all circumstances of life. Our clinical experience shows that the seemingly gratuitous effects observed in neurotics—their exaggerated hatred, love, pity, and other emotions—are the result of transferences; their unconscious fantasies reconnect ancient events and people who have long been forgotten with present circumstances. The displacement of the affective energy (linked to unconscious representations) to their actual ideas leads to exaggerated emotions. The "extreme behavior" of hysterics is well known, drawing both sarcasm and disdain; but since the time of Freud we know that it is to us, the doctors, that this sarcasm should be addressed for we have not recognized the symbolic depth of hysteria, resembling illiterates in the face of that meaningful and rich language.[47]

We can see it every day; a transference is the unconscious replaying of a conflict that was once repressed and forgotten. It encapsulates unfinished stories which alienate us and prevent us from truly living in the present reality.

Although transferences won't allow an individual to heal from an unintegrated story, they do provide temporary relief. Like a pressure cooker releasing steam, if the unconscious conflict is not integrated, then it will release itself in some external conflicts. Indeed, transferring old

---

[47] Sándor Ferenczi (1908), « Transfert et introjection », in *Psychanalyse I*, Payot, Paris, (1968).

events to present-day situations serves as an outlet for unconscious, internal conflicts. The latter is simply transferred into external conflicts, using concrete things or issues that correspond more or less to the internal ones. This dynamic can also be observed on a collective level, for example, with the need of some communities to produce pariahs and scapegoats.

In Depth Psychology, it is customary to explain that what is pushed out through the door comes back through the window. Lacan puts it like this, "what is foreclosed from the symbolic, reappears in the real."[48] An ancient wise man would also point out how the whole of society evades its psychological challenges by using medications, repression, and denial. As a result, it's not surprising that various crises—such as terrorist attacks, migration challenges, climate disruption, and environmental pollution—emerge, often bringing to light unresolved issues that were not integrated. A source of alienation

I suggest defining *transferential need* as a consequence of failed integration. Because conflictual experiences are not integrated, they can't find their place in a person's history. Consequently, they remain present, repressed or transferred onto aspects of the present day. This leads to these conflicts becoming crystallized in external relationships, distancing the individual from their true self, and hindering any introspective work. For example, someone suffering from paranoia might keep reliving an unconscious (but not unreal) trauma, constantly projecting it onto various aspects of the present day.

Aldo Naouri gives an example of incomplete mourning responsible for the transferential need a young

---

[48] In Lacanian theory, "foreclosure" (or "forclusion" in French) is a specific type of psychic mechanism where something fundamental is excluded from the symbolic order (such as language). This exclusion leads to its reappearance in the "real," which refers to the domain of material reality and experiences.

mother projected onto her baby. She had been harassing her pediatrician for several weeks on account of some minor issues involving her newborn child. These issues in no way justified her anguish. Finally, on a visit to the pediatrician, she told the doctor of a terrible nightmare she had just had. In the dream she saw the head of her son placed on a table, crying, and she could hear nothing. The young mother went on to say, "All of a sudden, I woke up. I went to my son's room. I turned on the light. He was asleep. And do you know what I did? I am sure I must be crazy. I woke him up and shook him until he cried. Then, when I heard his cries, I tried to calm him down. My husband woke up, but I didn't tell him about my dream. After that, I spent a long time rocking Samuel, trying to get him to fall back to sleep. I haven't slept since."[49]

Aldo Naouri tells us what happened next at the consultation: "Without going into detail about the content of her dream, Mrs Judith told me how she met Samuel's father, about their marriage, her pregnancy, and finally the birth of their son. Finally, she revealed that at that very moment, her father was dying on another floor of the same clinic, without her knowing it at the time. She was told of this two days later when the funeral—which she could not attend given her condition—was taking place. 'The more I think about it the crazier I feel, the more I try not to think about it, the more it comes back to me despite myself. One leaving, one being born, and me in the middle. Me? All by myself? I didn't choose the moment. Life chose it for me. How could I have known? They hid everything from me! And yet, even if they had told me, what could I have done? So, it keeps coming back to me, no matter what I'm thinking about I can't stop thinking about it. It's enough to drive you crazy."

---

[49] Aldo Naouri (1985), *Une place pour le père,* Seuil, Paris.

This situation describes how difficult it was for her to integrate the death of her father, "enough to drive you crazy" as she said. Several factors account for this difficulty. The fact that people hid the event from her, that it coincided with her giving birth, and that both events were going on in the same establishment. Because of this, the non-integrated event and its emotional charge were projected onto the newborn child, by attributing to him all sorts of problems, which were exaggerated for the most part. In this given scenario, she was expressing her own transferential needs. She had displaced the lack of integration of her father's death onto something outside of herself; onto the space between her and her child. The nightmare, as well as the possibility of talking about it and getting understanding from her pediatrician, most fortuitously enabled her to reconnect with the source of the problem. She could then integrate it instead of continuing to project it onto her newborn child, who had not been recognized for who he truly was.

Analyzing transferential needs

As the above examples show, transferential needs can prevent a person from recognizing others for who they truly are. In our daily lives, we can observe a great deal of energy and frustration in exchanges between people, as everyone tries to have their true self recognized. The challenge is that we try to defend ourselves from individuals who unconsciously and systematically project their unfinished stories onto us, putting us at risk of being alienated by them. But anyone who knows themselves understands the futility of this kind of argument and avoids it.

Rainer Maria Rilke (Malte) illustrates this type of adaptation of children towards the most intimate desires of the adult. He explains how, when he was a child, he managed to make his mother happy by playing the role of a little girl who had probably passed away, and that his mother seemed to be longing for. “It was only when we were very certain that we would not be disturbed, when night fell, that we would surrender ourselves to our memories, to old memories that we both shared, and which made us smile. We remembered the time when Mom wanted me to be a little girl and not the boy that, oh my God, I had to be. I cannot remember how I had guessed this, and I had the idea to knock on my mom’s door sometimes in the afternoon. When she asked who was there, I was happy to say from outside, "Sophie," in a voice so convincing that it tickled the back of my throat. And when I entered the room in my little indoor outfit with the sleeves rolled up, almost like a girl’s nightdress, I simply became Sophie. I was the little Sophie who took up so much of Mom’s thoughts and whose hair my mother would braid, so as not to confuse her with the naughty Malte if ever he came back. It pleased both Mom and Sophie that Malte stayed away, and their conversations—which Sophie carried on using the same high-pitched voice—consisted mainly of enumerating the misdeeds of Malte and complaining about him.”

This type of adaptation to another person’s transferential needs can become a real gilded prison. Malte could find himself forced to play the role of Sophie each time he wanted to establish a harmonious relationship with his mother, or later even with a partner.

Certain prejudices or ideals are transferential needs that shape not only cultures but also families and individuals. They operate in a dual space, wrapped up in an unconscious temporality, and manifest as incessant conflict. In therapy, we analyze several types of transference: those projected onto a person—sometimes even before their conception—and those that the person, in turn, unconsciously duplicates. Often, the therapist supports these projections hoping to be able to manage them effectively.

When analyzed, these transferences can unveil the dynamics of the unconscious and offer a way out from endless repetition. Therefore, it is important to address these transferences before the end of therapeutic work. Classical healing experiences in Depth Psychology offer important and rich teachings on the ways in which transferential needs work and how to analyze them.

In the following chapter, the integration of transferential needs will be further developed. This process can be understood as bringing about a change of focus towards introspection. Instead of using projections and transferences as a defense mechanism, the person identifies the underlying sources of these projections within themselves, thus progressively stopping them. This change is particularly likely when current issues can be associated with the family's history.

Transgenerational integration is about learning to turn our eyes inward to develop a dialogue between the inner and the outer world. From that perspective, family tree analysis provides a great tool for getting started. Additionally, a professional therapist's support can make a difference thanks to their ability to listen and to understand the unconscious of the patient. By doing so, a therapist can help the patient to step back from their current difficulties and start to adopt a different point of view, one that takes into consideration their unconscious reality. This introspective work allows the person to re-center themselves. Therefore, the more one understands oneself, the less the transferential needs of others will affect them.

5
Facing Transferential Needs

Now that I have introduced what is at the source of transgenerational transmissions—transferential needs—we can further look at them from the point of view of someone who inherits these failed integrations.

For the recipient, the one who is located "downstream" from the transmissions, there are several possible reactions. First and foremost, there is the possibility that they will integrate the other persons' transferential needs. However, if the receiver is unable to integrate them, they will resort to using defense mechanisms. These defensive reactions do not free the receiver from the problem. In the long run, they may become standard attitudes that alienate them. Two extreme reactions, the *nirvana style* and the *persona* are observable and will now be presented in more detail.

The nirvana style

The *nirvana style* refers to the tendency to repeat unfinished stories; to play them out, most often unconsciously. Secrets, omissions, shameful events, unthinkable acts, and emotional dramas are among the many elements that the *nirvana style* can unconsciously bring into play, generally to one's disadvantage.

Engaged in the work of transgenerational integration, Valerie told me of a memory she had that corresponded to my definition of the *nirvana style*. As she pictured her mother's childhood, and her Armenian grandparents' life after the genocide—at the beginning of the communist

Russian regime—she suddenly remembered an amazing episode of her own childhood. During a Sunday outing with her parents on the *Promenade des Anglais* in Nice, she remembered crying when she caught sight of two policemen in uniform. In an attempt to calm her down, they approached her, only causing her to scream even more, as she accused them of being "assassins." In hindsight, Valerie understood that at that specific moment, she was expressing emotion and rage connected to the unfinished stories of her grandparents, her mother, and a whole community that had been oppressed by men in uniforms.

Françoise Dolto writes of an event that also demonstrates how a little girl, through her actions, was replaying a non-integrated event that originally belonged to her parents. Her parents had requested a consultation because she had stopped speaking several years ago. During the first consultation, Dolto interpreted the little girl's game, as she repeatedly mimed dragging a doll from her mother's womb. She asked the parents if the mother had suffered any miscarriages since their daughter had been born, as this seemed to be what the child was miming with her doll. In response to the parents' surprise, the psychoanalyst explained that she was only interpreting their daughter's actions, which seemed to imitate a miscarriage. Agreeing to break their silence, the parents talked about this event that they had, until then, kept secret. In doing so, they released their daughter of the burden of their own transferential needs, freeing her from the muteness from which she had been suffering. This is a good example of the *nirvana style*: by miming her mother's miscarriage, the daughter represented an experience that her parents had not integrated. Once her parents acknowledged their experience and spoke about it, the child was liberated from the weight of their unconscious projection, which had caused her muteness.

Guy Ausloss presents another example showing how the *nirvana style* can symbolically repeat unfinished stories, so that they may finally be spoken out. "I would like to illustrate this with an example taken from a family in which the child had an unusual taste for blood and weapons which he avidly collected. One night, he assaulted a fifty-year-old man in the toilet of a café with one of the knives from his collection and demanded money from him. The man managed to escape and call the police but so did the teenager. When the police arrived, he claimed that he had been sexually abused. However, his statements were inconsistent, and his story did not hold up, leading the judge to place him in protective custody." Later, the whole family received treatment by a team of family therapists. The parents complained about not being able to have private meetings, for "they had things to say which they could not say in front of the children." Ausloss recounts what the father of the adolescent had told him: "During the Second World War, his own father killed a German soldier. Although this act seemed almost without justification in that chaotic period—where killing an enemy soldier could be seen as part of the resistance—it had severe consequences. Such actions often led to reprisals, including hostage-taking and executions. The story took a dramatic turn when the man was denounced by his own father, presumably to prevent said retaliations. He ended up in a concentration camp, and his son was raised by the grandfather. This fostered deep resentment and violence between the grandfather and the grandson. This inherited violence culminated in the great-grandson, the adolescent, assaulting a 50-year-old man, symbolically stepping into his father's role and enacting the aggression his father could not direct at his own grandfather."[50]

---

[50] Guy Ausloss (1980), "Œdipe et sa famille, ou les secrets sont faits pour être agis", in *Dialogue*, n°70, AFCCC, Paris.

This example shows that the teenager had to act out so that his parents would talk about these dramatic events that had never been integrated. This young man's alienation and the weight of his parent's transferential needs were expressed through his *nirvana style.*

In similar ways, certain life events of the French poet Arthur Rimbaud refer to forms of alienation also expressed through a *nirvana style*. More specifically, Alain de Mijolla[51] noticed how the memory of the poet's father haunted him. Rimbaud used to say he was fleeing the military police because he was a deserter from the 47th Infantry Regiment; however, he had never been in the military, and the 47th Regiment was the one his father had belonged to.

We find another example of nirvana style in Philippe Grimbert's book *Secret*.[52] There, he explains that during his childhood, he had made a habit of setting the table for an imaginary friend, without ever knowing at that time that his parents had lost a firstborn son, and that they had never properly grieved this loss.

In instances of acting out, as well as in psychotic or 'borderline' episodes that often seem inexplicable, we may uncover signs of unconscious, transgenerational influences. Didier Dumas notes that "psychotic children seem to have a relentless mission to heal their family's past. They are exceptional explorers of the transgenerational unconscious. These children express or recount things which at first make no sense to others. However, when we listen to them seriously; it becomes clear that they are exploring a family past that has shaped who they are. It's as if they spend much of their time navigating their parent's unconscious, searching for long-lost loves—

---

[51] Alain de Mijolla (1981), *Les visiteurs du moi*, Les Belles Lettres, Paris.

[52] Philippe Grimbert (2012), *Secret*, Granta Books, NY.

whether they be grandparents or great-aunts and uncles whom the parent or their parent could never fully grieve."[53]

Beyond the parental relation and its possible sterile moralization, transgenerational analysis of "psychotic" symptoms allows us to eventually discover and give meaning to the situation, and from there, to envision integration and healing. Irrational behaviors also teach us about the general functioning of the *nirvana style,* which is not limited to psychotic or masochistic manifestations. It can appear in all of us in certain contexts, such as under the influence of alcohol, drugs, or medication. It is also present in those who, in response to familial or collective norms, become shaped or confined by a mold in the name of "normality". This can bring them to create their own families and engage in apparently ideal lives, without being able to address their issues, which may then be projected and unconsciously transmitted onto their children. However, transgenerational analysis is not a matter of making moral judgments. It is about seeing things as they are[54]to reach a point of lucidity that will bring us beyond appearances, beyond explanations, unveiling the hidden meanings of our transgenerational heritages.

On the creative side

Charles Perrault, the author of many children's tales, dealt with several incomplete bereavements in his family, most notably concerning an older sister and a twin brother. Without conscious intention, he inserted these family shortcomings between the lines of his writing. For

---

[53] Nina Canault (1998), *Comment paye-t-on les fautes de ses ancêtres?*, Desclée de Brouwer, Paris.

[54] This is, of course, the whole difference between the standard, positivist, explanatory approaches in psychology, and my phenomenological approach in Depth Psychology on unconscious meanings - which I will briefly present in the eighth chapter.

instance, in *Sleeping Beauty*, there is the incongruous arrival of an old witch at the same moment the fairy godmothers are gathered around the cradle of a newborn child. Nicolas Abraham and Maria Torok have shown that for the psyche, the figure of the old witch corresponds to the unconscious, dark side of the family, their unfinished stories as well as their unintegrated griefs. According to Denise Morel, the crypt harbors incomplete mourning and brings together several deaths over several generations. "Not only did Charles Perrault refer to his twin (who died at age six) and to his sister Marie (the only girl amongst the brothers and who died aged thirteen), he also referred to other deaths that shaped the lives of his parents and earlier generations, where mourning was not sufficiently elaborated. [...] In the fairy tale, the crypt appears symbolically in the form of an inaccessible place where the young princess lay sleeping for a hundred years!"[55] Perrault notes that "the king and queen, after having kissed their dear child without waking her, leave the castle and published a prohibition to prevent anyone from approaching it. However, this was not necessary. Within a quarter of an hour, a great quantity of trees, of interlocking brambles and thorns grew around the park such that neither beast nor man would be able to get through them. [...] All the Perrault children, however curious and avidly interested they might be, and however tormented, did not need a parental prohibition explicitly forbidding them to explore the obscure regions of their family histories, because in these families, as in so many others, the impenetrable crypts made themselves felt by all kinds of symptoms."

Whether presented in a symptomatic or artistic form (or both), these various ways to stage transgenerational

---

[55] Denise Morel-Ferla (2015), « Les fantômes de la famille Perrault », dans *Analyses transgénérationnelles pour mieux comprendre*, ouvrage collectif, Genesis Editions, Geneva.

heritages are at the heart of what I call the *nirvana style*. Without even suspecting it, the person remains a prisoner of their alienations and intimately related to the unresolved stories of their ancestors. They unconsciously seek to bring to light these unfinished stories that they need to integrate.

Family secrets seep out between the lines of many other authors. For example, Serge Tisseron identified the presence of a family secret in Hergé's work. By analyzing the *Tintin* comic books, the uncanny resemblance between the family names of Thomson and Thompson, and the character of Castafiore who systematically forgets the name of Captain Haddock, we are presented with some clues that reveal a secret about the paternal lineage of the author, Hergé. Tisseron explains that "there are many strange occurrences in *Tintin*. There is the resemblance between Thomson and Thomspon (who are not brothers), Captain Haddock's transformation over the years, and the almost incomprehensible denouement of certain stories, such as the resolution of *Red Rackham's Treasure*... By studying all of these bizarre incidents, I became convinced that a second secret story lurked behind those of Hergé's characters and that this illusion masked the sufferings of a boy born of an unknown, yet illustrious father."[56]

Tisseron also recalls, "When I presented my hypothesis in 1981, we knew nothing of Hergé's life. It might have not gone any further. However, a few years later, some journalists discovered that a family secret did exist! His father, Alexis Remi, was, in fact, born of an unknown father, probably of illustrious origins! In addition, more plot twists were further revealed: Hergé's father had a twin

[56] Serge Tisseron (1992), *Tintin et les secrets de famille*, Aubier, Paris.

brother named Léon, and they were both raised in middle-class families. A countess, living in a real castle, had offered to pay for their clothes and their education!"

Serge Tisseron explains that, in Hergé's work, the Thom(p)son represent his father and uncle. They are investigators, in search of a truth that repeatedly escapes them, similar to how a son may unconsciously search for his biological father. In addition, we have Bianca Castafiore who keeps a secret that she refuses to unveil. "Castafiore doesn't stop talking for the sake of talking. It's as if she doesn't want to risk being questioned on a subject that is too sensitive for her. She never answers questions directly. Isn't this exactly what someone trying to keep a secret would do? Finally, there is one particular element meant to create confusion: the name of the Captain. In *The Calculus Affair*, Bianca Castafiore is speaking to Tintin when she cannot remember Captain Haddock's name: "Ah! Little flatterer, you came to congratulate me as well as this... this fisherman... Mr? ... Mr? [...]". And in another comic, *The Castafiore Emerald,* she repeatedly calls him Kappock (p.8), Koddack (p.9), Mastock, Kosack (p.10), Kolback, Karbock (p. 22), Karnack (p. 23), Hablock (p. 34), Maggock (p. 55), Medock and Kapstock (p. 56)!"[57]

This famous interpretation by Serge Tisseron shows how family secrets can be echoed by those who inherit them. Furthermore, it indicates that there is a deep unconscious desire to shed light on these unfinished stories, so that they may one day be integrated.

Some artists have not had a chance to meet success during their lives and emancipate themselves through their artistic production. Vincent Van Gogh[58] and Camille

---

[57] Interview appearing in the Journal *Psychologie* (april 1999).

[58] Alves-Périé Élisabeth (2015) « Les Van Gogh : des gens très bien », dans *Analyses transgénérationnelles pour mieux comprendre, tome 1*, ouvrage collectif, Genesis Editions, Geneva.

Claudel[59] tried unsuccessfully to overcome an alienation stemming from parents who had not been able to mourn the death of an earlier child. The intensity of their effort testifies to the pain they suffered from not being recognized for who they are—their true Self. These two artists unconsciously battled against the legacy of their parents' unaccomplished mourning, without being able to discover the source of their alienation. The sculptures of Camille Claudel, her transference onto Rodin (reproducing the alienation with respect to her mother), her need for recognition, and her abortion, all reflect her attempts to connect with her mother. These events, within the broader context of her family dynamics, highlight her efforts to address the unresolved grief of her mother's idealized first-born son.

The fate of the painter Gustave Courbet is an example of what may happen to a replacement child when unconscious conflicts are over-exacerbated. In an article[60] based on his life, I wrote more about his outstanding family heritage. Not only was Gustave Courbet the replacement child of an older brother, but also of two uncles (one maternal and one paternal) who died young, both of whom were the expected heirs of their respective families. Thanks to his artistic genius and the passion he put into his work; he had long overcome this issue. However, despite his international success, he always suffered from a lack of recognition—specifically because he was a replacement child, part of an unconscious problem that was never fully integrated. He needed to be unique, different from others, whatever the price. That is why, he broke

---

[59] « Camille Claudel rattrapée par son héritage transgénérationnel » in *Analyses transgénérationnelles pour mieux comprendre, tome 1*, Genesis Editions, Geneva.

[60] « Gustave Courbet, entre ombre et lumières » in *Analyses transgénérationnelles pour mieux comprendre*, tome 2, 2020, Genesis Editions, Geneva.

many rules, did not follow academic guidelines, and painted scandalous nudes (such as the famous *Origin of the World*). But eventually, his luck ran out. After the revolt of *The Commune* in Paris, Gustave Courbet was judged responsible for the destruction of the famous *Vendôme Column*. Branded as an outcast, and as an unwanted child (when not in his replacement role), he fled the country, and it was only after his death that his body was returned to France and his reputation restored by his homeland.

We can therefore understand how certain artistic activities serve as attempts to draw attention to these hidden legacies. Creative compulsion can also act as a defense against the transferential needs of others. Here, the compulsive need to make discoveries and to produce novelties, attest to a deep desire to rid himself of alienating unfinished stories.

The "nirvana principle"

Like the visible part of an iceberg that floats on deep water, the *nirvana style* manifests the apparent side of an individual, who is drowned in a fusional and alienating space, in the symbolic womb of his parents. The *Nirvana style* can be understood as the fruit, or outcome, of the "nirvana principle," which we need to understand if we want to facilitate change and healing. Freud[61] refers to this "nirvana principle" as a natural biological and psychological disposition, which tends towards a state of lesser excitement. In this context, he speaks of a fantasy of returning to our intra-uterine origins, accompanied by an "oceanic" feeling of well-being.

---

[61] Freud saw in nirvana the absence of excitation: "It is known that we have found in the tendency towards reduction, to consistency, to the suppression of internal tension, the dominant tendency of the life of the psyche and perhaps of neurological life in general (the Nirvana principal to use the expression of Barbara Low)." Sigmund Freud, (1920), *Beyond the Pleasure Principle*, Norton, NY.

As I have shown in the preceding examples, a child who responds (unconsciously) to the needs of their mother may forget themself and remain fused with her. A child is not aware of what it means to be a distinct Self, they may easily be trapped in a fusional relation that prevents them from becoming an individuated Self. The term "nirvana" is appropriate to refer to this lack of care about oneself, while pacifying the relationship with the suffering parent. With Michel Richard, we may recall the "primal scene" psychoanalysts have analyzed. When a child experiences repeated humiliation, deprivation, and rejection, they may come to conclude, "I have no hope of being loved for who I am." At this point, the child is likely to develop neurosis, as they begin to behave according to the expectations of their parents or others, rather than following their own desires."[62]

This helps us understand why an adult or a child might take on the "transferential necessity" of another person, such as a parent. By shouldering this burden, the individual creates a kind of smokescreen for the original sufferer (like the parent), allowing the non-integrated conflict to be projected onto something else, thus providing the sufferer a sense of relief. To clarify, when a transferential need finds a way to project itself, the unconscious conflicts and their symptoms are eased, which improves the quality of one's relations with those around them. However, once this type of relation is put in place, it leaves no room for the person on whom the transferential needs falls to become their Self. Self-abnegation, which gives way to a less conflictual relationship, ultimately becomes a source of lasting alienation. This is where the *nirvana style* finds its roots. It prioritizes the relationship's well-being over the development of one's real Self, hoping to one day be freed

[62] Michel Richard, (1998), *Les courants de la psychologie*, Chroniques Sociales, Lyon, p. 168.

from this unconscious function. However, this is rarely the case. Sándor Ferenczi[63] had studied this type of dynamic and recognized that "fear [...] turns children into psychiatrists, so to speak."

Integrating the nirvana style

Nirvana style emancipation relies on the correct interpretation of the meaning behind these unconscious behaviors and other symptomatic manifestations. When these symptoms can be associated with some events in the life of an ancestor, the person can stop identifying with them and start to discover the true origins of their symptoms. This expanded awareness allows the individual to gradually understand the significance of their symptoms, leading to a clearer sense of self and a greater distinction from their alienations.

Here is an example in which a dream analysis brings out this differentiation between the Self and the alienated parts. Paul asked to consult because of severe insomnia, fatigue due to lack of sleep, and an obsession with serious existential questioning. Among his obsessive topics, Paul would question his relationship with his girlfriend. Would he be happier in another relationship, with his flirtatious yoga teacher, who seemed "kind" and understanding? By shedding light on his ancestors' history, we discovered the extent to which a negative representation of heterosexual men was present on his mother's side of the family. When they were young, both his grandmother and her sister had been abused by a family member, without this ever being acknowledged or spoken about. The grandmother also appeared to have hidden the identity of the biological father of her first daughter Joelle (the older sister of Paul's mother). She married quickly and forced her husband to remain silent about not being the true father. The secret

---

[63] Sándor Ferenczi, *Psychanalyse*, IV, Payot, 1982, Paris, p. 133.

she kept had profound repercussions for the entire family, which had grown up in a severe and bigoted atmosphere. Was Joelle's complicated relationship with her father figure related to her later experiences and identity? How can one trust a man if the person meant to be your father is cheating you? Joelle remained bound by the secret and died young from cancer, never learning the truth about her origins. The second sister also suffered from the family secret; she had an unhappy marriage and ultimately committed suicide. It was only much later that the grandmother shared her secret with her other children, including Paul's mother. When Paul's parents got divorced, his father was blamed, reinforcing Paul's negative view of men. In his family, it seemed heterosexual men were not to be trusted: they abused teenage girls, got women pregnant, pretended to be biological fathers when they weren't and seemed unable to be adequate husbands.

By clarifying the unspoken stories of his forefathers, Paul gained awareness of his unconscious transgenerational legacies. Gradually, he differentiates the lives of his ancestors from his own. As he learned to listens to himself, he manages to differentiate himself from them and move closer to who he is.

Analyzing his dreams was an important part of his journey towards integration and self-understanding. Paul recounted two particularly significant dreams: "I dreamed that a close friend confided in me that he was gay. I asked him why he had married, and he explained that it was the perfect cover, as no one would suspect his true sexual identity. I felt a sense of relief, realizing that I had been grappling with his questions as if they were my own. In reality, these concerns belonged to him, not me."

In another dream, Paul associated his insomnia with his maternal grandmother: "I was with a childhood friend, a former childhood crush of mine with whom I had caught up recently, and I told her that I was no longer with my partner, that we had split up. She was happy for me and perhaps, for herself too, given that we could now begin a romantic relationship. We found ourselves in a shop, and in the corner of this shop, there was a bed. We got in, and I held her close. She told me I had smooth skin. It felt nice to feel her curves and her soft skin. I felt a sense of happiness between us. Later, when we talked about going to sleep, she told me that she had insomnia, and I told her that it probably wasn't a good idea to go to my maternal great-grandmother's house because there was only a small bed there, and I wouldn't sleep well if she had insomnia and moved all through the night. I was relieved that it was not me who had insomnia, but someone else." Paul was able to see that his dreams represented a differentiation between himself, and what alienated him from "other's" unfinished stories which mirrored his ancestors' issues. Such a differentiation revealed the transferential needs of his entourage, which until now, remained unsuspected. He could now begin working on integrating these transferential needs, instead of replaying them in the form of a *nirvana style*.

Nicolas Abraham and Maria Torok give an example of the interpretation of some seemingly inexplicable behaviors, which also helped people to differentiate themselves from their alienation. "One of us analyzed a boy who 'carried' his older sister, who before dying towards the age of eight, had "seduced" him. When the boy reached puberty, he began to steal women's undergarments. After a long analysis, a providential slip of the tongue—in which he confused his age with the age his sister would have had if she had been alive—enabled us to reconstruct his internal situation and the reason for his 'kleptomania'. To explain his stealing, he said 'when she was fourteen, she would have needed a bra.' The young boy's crypt sheltered the little girl, keeping her 'alive'. He was unconsciously keeping track of her maturing process."[64]

Although the terms used by these authors differ somewhat from my own, this situation demonstrates clearly how the thefts of women's undergarments "spoke" of the uncompleted mourning of his sister. By acting as his adolescent sister would have acted had she not died, the *nirvana style* that was put into play demonstrates the source of his alienation. Similarly, Philippe Grimbert[65] in one of his books shows how an unconscious transgenerational heritage pushed an adult into buying a child's dress, without any rational reason to do so.

The Persona

Now let us look at another way in which we can respond to transferential needs. I have borrowed the word *persona* from the classical vocabulary to define a form of alienation which takes the opposite approach from the *nirvana style.* While the *nirvana style* is the result of a fusional and alienating relationship, the *persona* is defined as cutting one's Self off from the relationship. As we will find out, by cutting one's Self off from a relationship, the *persona* also cuts off a part of himself, notably the true Self in him. The consequences of such a rupture are therefore of great significance. Although the *persona* ends conflictual relationships by casting them aside, other problems emerge. The conflictual relationship a parent harbors, for example, may become the source of a new transferential need that the child might project onto another person (such as a sibling). Instead of addressing the underlying transferential need, the persona simply shifts it onto someone else. This creates a cycle where unresolved issues

---

64 Nicolas Abraham and Maria Torok, *The Shell and the Kernel*, 1994, University of Chicago Press.

65 Philippe Grimbert (2001), *La petite robe de Paul*, Grasset & Flasquelle, Paris.

are transferred and multiplied, much like a domino effect. For instance, the way a superior's grievances are passed down to subordinates in a hierarchical organization.

Etymologically the word *persona* means a theatrical mask as well as the "role attributed to a mask". Not only does the mask separate the impersonal from the authentic, but it also covers up the expressions of life (movements made by the face), substituting it for a fixed appearance, like time standing still, or death. Here the shell takes the place of the kernel. This definition of the word *persona* emphasizes the tendency to disinvest the deep Self, and distance one's Self from who one truly is.

Jung[66] had already used the term *persona* to account for the influence of the "collective psyche" on the individual. He presented the *persona* as a kind of graft added onto the authentic Self. I suggest that we also look at it as a form of unconscious alienation, which can be as much familial, as it can be collective, or cultural. Following the model of the *superego*, which is considered an entity grafted onto the pure psyche of a child, the *persona* can be regarded as a more general form of alienation, sometimes cultural. While the *persona* is often the fruit of a collective influence, it can also arise from an alienation pertaining more specifically to a family, or even from a two-person relationship, such as between a mother and child.

Therefore, when faced with a transferential need that has not been successfully integrated, the *persona* generates a new transferential need and possibly amplifies it. In this way, the *persona* contributes to the perpetuation of the failures of integration and renders their restoration even more complicated. On a collective scale, the *persona* can take a cultural form, patriarchy, and matriarchy for exam-

---

[66] Carl Gustav Jung (1964), *The Collected Works of C. G. Jung*, Routledge, 2015, NY.

ple. In his analysis of the diverse forms of the development of the personality, Jung wrote: "The possibilities of the developments described in the previous chapters are basically, when closely examined, so many *alienations from oneself*—partial depersonalization as it were, sometimes for the benefit of an exterior role, sometimes for the benefit of an imagined or imaginary importance."

To account for interferences that may occur between the kernel and the shell, or between the true Self and his *persona,* professional literature refers to terms such as "crypt" in reference to incomplete bereavements, "delusions of being possessed", "inclusion", "conservative repression", or "split personality", to designate variations of this kind of psyche's division. The term that best describes an individual's persona can vary, depending on several factors, particularly the extent to which transgenerational legacies have been amplified over multiple generations Consequently, neurotic states found in a first generation can explain the use of denial in the second generation. Claude Béran and Dominique De Vargas[67] have noted this aspect in the case of sexual perverts. It is indeed well known that many abusers repeat the mistreatment they have experienced themselves as victims. With the limited language they have at their disposal, they attribute the "inexplicable" activities they are guilty of to "someone else inside them." These denials of reality correspond to some archaic defensive mechanism. They transfer onto someone else their own unbearable experiences, a tendency very often observed among sadists, manipulators, and perverts.

The literature often discusses the recognition of sexual differences and the challenges related to heterosexual and

---

[67] Claude Béran and Dominique De Vargas (2002), "Chronique d'une session de groupe avec des auteurs d'abus sexuels", in *Psychiatrie et violence* n°12, Forensic, Paris.

Oedipal dynamics. Transgenerational analysis can shed light on how inherited traumas might affect individuals' sexual and romantic lives. For some teenagers, navigating heterosexual relationships may be complicated if their parents have unresolved conflicts about their own or their ancestors' sexual traumas or experiences.

Integrating the Persona

In general, and in contrast to the *nirvana style*, the *persona* does not suffer from a lack of societal recognition or a bad reputation. Its mask allows it to safely navigate the world of appearances. However, the *persona* suffers from being disconnected from the Self within, without even knowing it. This is a common problem experienced by many, which Freud identified as a collective neurosis he analyzed in the famous "Civilization and its Discontent."[68]

At the cultural level, the *persona* usually conforms to the transferential needs of the collective and makes them its own, for example always being politically correct. How long can this kind of adaptation substitute for the need to deepen one's sense of being and to blossom as one's true Self? In this context, it is important to understand that the symptoms an individual may present are calls to question oneself and to return to one's true Self. The presence of symptoms indicates a degree of individualization[69] of the *persona*, revealing aspects that set it apart from others. A process of humanization is to render and mitigate the psychological solitude that the *persona* unconsciously suffers.

Because it functions as a defense mechanism, the *persona* is designed to project its failures of integration where appearances best lend themselves to it. The problem is not

---

[68] "Das Unbehagen in der Kultur» translated as « Civilization and its Discontent ».

[69] It is indeed in this respect that the symptoms should not be artificially suppressed without some meaningful counterpart in return.

recognized as one's own, but rather as something external, another person, the environment, a part of one's body, and so on. As we have seen in a case described by Aldo Naouri, it may be similarly derived from a grief that proved too difficult to mourn, or anguish which a mother projects onto so-called symptoms exhibited by her newborn child. It is a very common way of operating that projects outside of the proper reasons why something does not work: an unfair social system, someone guilty of causing trouble in the family, difficult economic conditions, a nasty neighbor, a hot climate, etc. Of course, difficult realities, even tragic ones, do exist. However, those who do nothing but project their own unconscious conflicts on existing problems, stand no chance of solving them. To delegate one's problems to others creates nothing but a vicious downward spiral, in which the failures of integration are amplified, leading to an increasing disinvestment of the Self.

Therapeutic work tends to overcome these never-ending transferential processes. For example, Salomon Sellam describes the positive consequences a teenage girl experienced once her mother allowed herself to take off her mask and talk about her inner world. The teenager, who always wore black and was fascinated by the gothic movement, felt misunderstood by her peers and had trouble in school and with her friends. In recounting the family history, the mother talked about an abortion that had taken place before her daughter was born. "I was marked for life by the experience; there was no compassion in the clinic. From the way the doctor spoke to me, I felt as if I had committed murder. I regretted it for a long time." Salomon Sellam explains that while the mother was talking, a strong emotion came over her. Her chin trembled, and she began to cry. Witnessing this, he asked her to describe the thoughts she had had at that time. "In my mind, I had committed murder, and I desperately wanted to make amends. My daughter was born two years after the abortion. I felt like I had made amends for this crime, and I did not speak about it to anyone." The insight she had about the relationship between this non-integrated event, and her daughter's difficulties opened a therapeutic window. "I always felt that my first child was still there by my side. Because of that, I was never really able to create room for my daughter. For me, that first pregnancy was my oldest child, and they were still alive in my thoughts. I used to imagine them growing up and going to school, playing sports, studying, etc. They were virtual." Some months later, the mother talked about how her daughter "had made lots of friends and had rediscovered her *joie de vivre*. My husband and I can't believe it!"[70]

This example shows how, by voicing this previously non-integrated event, the mother relieved her daughter of the weight of this transferential need. By giving up her *persona*, she freed her daughter from a legacy that her daughter had been re-enacting through a *nirvana style*, and which prevented her normal development.

Conclusion

Each of us can be understood as being made up of a mix of *persona*, *nirvana style*, and our true Self. In keeping with our transgenerational legacies, our entourage, and current conditions (and based upon the state of Self-development), we react to our experiences without necessarily being able to work through them and integrate them. Therefore, it is not unusual for an individual, in intimate settings, to behave according to a certain *nirvana style*, for example behaving childishly due to early frustrations, while in public, they display a more politically correct *persona*.

---

[70] Salomon Sellam (2007), *Le syndrome du gisant*, Bérangel, Saint-André-de-Sagonis, p.262-263.

Integration work helps an individual to analyze the meaning of their *nirvana style*. It also allows individuals to better understand their transferential needs and their *personas* and then to decode their unconscious meanings. By allowing one's Self to talk freely, and by encouraging it to go beyond alienations, a return to the true Self is made possible.

Summary

Nirvana Style	Integration	Persona
The heir puts into play the story that has been projected onto them.	The Self integrates the transferential needs by symbolizing the relationship.	The heir disinvests their true Self and replicates a transferential need.
The *nirvana style* is a vain attempt to defend oneself against an alienating relationship.	The Self develops its own capacities for integration and emancipation.	The *persona* develops itself based on the failures of integration, the need of transference and the loss of one's true Self.
Obsessive creativity in the *nirvana style* reveals a refusal to be identified with the transferential needs of another.	This emancipation is achieved through a symbolization of the transfer of the other.	The *persona* develops an impersonal and collective discourse.

6
Transgenerational Integration

Integration does not only concern unconscious transgenerational heritages. Indeed, it is a very general psychological ability that enables us to give meaning to our life experiences. By integrating our daily life experiences, we are more likely to achieve a healthy psychological balance. On the contrary, when we fail to integrate events, we are left with the weight of these unfinished stories. If we try to repress or forget them, they will come back as symptoms, or they will be repeated, or transmitted to future generations.

In a sort of continuous updating of our lives, integration is a form of psychological work that comes naturally to us, like breathing or eating. Contrary to that modern maxim "stop thinking," we should learn to truly think for ourselves. Thinking is different from pondering the same ideas over and over again. Learning to think is also learning not to think. When we stop identifying with our mental representations, our true Self can provide a broader perspective. We must stop undervaluing the importance of creative thinking, the human intelligence that explores our relationship with life, and all attempts to assimilate new knowledge. Once we are beyond judgments, beliefs, explanations, stereotypes, and prejudices, our mind can take on a life of its own; filled with ideas, insights, and awareness that make our life experiences meaningful while re-enchanting the world.

Facing resistances

Rather than trying "not to think about it," one should learn how to think, ask the right questions, read, find a competent therapist, or traditionally, find masters or spiritual guides. This quest for truth, filled with "enigmas" to solve, is at the source of many discoveries, big and small; these have shaped humanity from the invention of the wheel to the modern new technologies that allow a solar plane to fly around the world.

Just as new ideas clash with ancient ones, truths are also confronted by many types of resistance. Galileo's view that the Earth revolved around the sun was strongly opposed (many thought it was the other way around), as was the idea that the Earth was round (and not flat).

In *Philoctetes*, Sophocles explains, "A good man must speak the truth and must suffer for it without taking offense." When you decide to unravel certain family stories, you should be prepared to encounter significant resistance, which can discourage you from continuing the journey. This resistance can stifle deeper thought, reducing it to mere facts and confining discussions to what is politically correct. This is what happens in families that only talk about the weather, or gossip about others, cultivating persona lifestyle.

But how can one inquire into the history of family members—parents, grandparents, uncles, and cousins—when they may unconsciously be entrenched in a culture of silence, taboo, and unspoken truths? How can one lift the veil of family secrets without exacerbating resistance or causing negative repercussions for oneself and future generations? Confronting these hidden aspects can provoke negative reactions, leading to increased resistance and potentially worsening the very issues one sought to resolve. This is precisely where a therapist provides a confidential space to navigate these complexities without being overly reliant on the family's response.

Instead of confronting family members head-on, it is better to first understand the resistances and the stakes tied to transgenerational legacies—family secrets, unresolved grief, traumas, and other stories that haunt the family and cultural unconscious. It is also important to be wary of superficial defense mechanisms, such as reacting by doing the opposite of what one's parents did. The therapeutic alternative is to embark on a new, creative path that transcends duality and pacifies history without fueling the original conflicts, as can sometimes be seen in certain political and ideological movements.

Reconnecting with the true self—becoming where the self is absent—is not a process that comes at the expense of others. It is not about judging or condemning, but about clarifying to integrate these legacies and, at times, opening a therapeutic path for other family members. This approach of pacifying history also addresses unconscious guilt, which often no longer has a place and dissipates once the original conflicts are understood within a broader context, including any earlier transgenerational legacies.

However, resistances are also internal, due for example, to our unconscious loyalties, which are often opposed to the idea of consulting a professional. But when the symptoms are stronger than the resistance, the motivation to confront the internal resistance makes the difference and the therapeutic work can begin.

Healing the lack of transmissions

Derived from the Latin *filius*, the term "filiation" usually refers to a relationship bounding a child to their parents. This link is as likely to be biological as it can be anthropological, juridical, psychological, or symbolic. When considering the integration of transgenerational heritages, it is, of course, the symbolic transmission that we need to consider, that of a parental edifying function, their "word", enabling the birth of the Self in the child.

As psychotherapy has demonstrated, the role of the parents cannot be reduced to a simple procreative function. The parental role also encompasses participating in the development of the true Self of the child. Didier Dumas, who has interpreted biblical symbolism, insists on the virtues of the spoken word, and the impact of symbolic deficiencies on the fate of new generations. Beginning with Cain and Abel, "The tragic destiny of the first two children is caused by nothing other than an enormous lack of speech because their parents had not conceived them in the same way that God had created the parents, first in words and second in the flesh. By presenting Men as an individual who was fabricated in two steps, the Bible proposes a precise model for the conception of a child. This model states that it is necessary to follow the way in which God conceived man and woman, first in speech and then in the flesh. In other words, it explains that the conception of a child is necessarily twofold, mental and physical, incorporeal and material. Psychoanalysis brings this to light daily, the words and fantasies with which our parents conceived us, mark us much more than the coitus in which they materialized their desire."[71]

This point of view on filiation is most interesting from the transgenerational analysis perspective; it implies that to give birth to the Self in the child, they should first exist on a symbolic and verbal level.[72] This strengthens the idea that the child depends on the parental "word" for the Self

[71] Didier Dumas (2001), *La Bible et ses fantômes*, de Brouwer, Paris.

[72] An ancient perspective that originates with the Egyptian god Ptah who created the world with his words (his *logos*).

to develop. Therapy will seek to restore this "verb" and to allow the integration of unconscious heritages.

A holistic approach

Integration should also be understood from a holistic perspective[73]. Thus, emotions and everything else that a conflictual relationship can bring up, are involved in integration work. And when we repeatedly fail to integrate, this will exacerbate our mood. By contrast, when meaning is given to a symptom, it will increase in energy. Gestalt therapists have noticed that a positive emotional impact is experienced by a patient when new awareness or insights are gained, both of which accompany the work of integration.

Integration mobilizes the whole of the psycho-affective sphere, namely: emotions, intelligence, intuition, creativity, the unconscious, etc. Moreover, if we accept the definition of intelligence as the ability to acquire new knowledge, then integration could be considered an essential form of intelligence. In their own way, slips of the tongue, dreams, and fantasies reveal unconscious complexes awaiting integration.

Didier Dumas provides an example attesting to the importance of understanding one's dreams to integrate transgenerational alienation. A woman had been consulting him for two years, unable to engage in sexual activity after the birth of her first child. Despite her love for her husband, she panicked at the slightest physical contact. It was clear that with the child's arrival, her husband had become, for her, "an untouchable father."

This situation was resolved thanks to her nightmares which involved violent scenes where newborn babies were put to death. "She had already explored her genealogy

---

73 Holistic comes from the Greek term *holos*, meaning "the whole."

four generations back without encountering any event connected to incomplete bereavement, which could usually explain symptoms such as the ones she was experiencing. As she continued her quest to find out if a family secret or another meaningful bit of information existed, she stumbled upon a discovery: `I found it! I spent the weekend at my parents' place and I found it! I asked my father about his childhood again and learned something I never knew about. My grandfather was not just married twice, but three times. Between my father's mother who died of typhus, and his stepmother, there was Aunt Odile. I had heard people talk about her, yet I did not know her personally. And since everybody called her Aunt Odile, I didn't know she'd been my grandfather's second wife. Their marriage lasted three years but she never managed to have children. According to my father, she had had five miscarriages." Didier Dumas then asked how old her father was. "Three or four years old. Grandpa remarried soon after the death of his first wife. He married the children's governess. He wanted to give my father and my aunts another mother. Their relationship probably began even before the death of my father's mother."[74]

Didier Dumas explains: "Marie-Hélène's dream suddenly became clear. She discovered that she had been haunted by the childhood fears of her father, for whom the series of infant deaths following his mother's passing had undoubtedly been a traumatic experience. She understood why, against all logic, she had abruptly developed a phobia of the man she had turned into a father." In other words, Didier Dumas's client was expressing, through her symptoms and her nightmares, a transgenerational heritage dating back to events that had marked her father's early childhood. This discovery allowed her to successfully integrate the problem she had with her husband.

---

[74] Didier Dumas (2000), *Et l'enfant créa le père,* Hachette, Paris.

I have often been able to confirm the importance of dreams and fantasies in accessing the unconscious realities underlying symptoms. For example, recalling nightmares during a consultation with a child allowed me to identify an incomplete mourning process. This child told me of a gold chain that he had inherited from his grandfather and that was of such importance to him that he never wanted to be without it. Beneath this object was his grandfather, whose loss the child had not yet grieved. The child's attitude towards this chain, as well as the omnipresent ghosts in his nightmares, reflected his position as the inheritor of an uncompleted bereavement, not yet integrated by his mother, and on the way to becoming his own. Once the origin of his nightmares was revealed, the child was able to share more details surrounding the death and burial of his grandfather, leading him to gradually integrate these life events.

Mythology and introspection

Mythology and its symbolic language help us to develop a dialogue with our unconscious, facilitating the integration process. Fairy tales also possess this symbolic quality that inspires the psyche and reawakens it without requiring belief or explanations. Bettelheim emphasized that "the child needs to understand what is happening in their conscience mind, and by extension to confront what is happening in their unconscious. This understanding, which helps them deal with their difficulties, is not gained through a rational analysis of the unconscious, but by becoming familiar with it—by engaging with daydreams and exploring fantasies derived from elements of fairy tales that resonate with their unconscious pressures. By doing so, the child transforms the content of their unconscious into fantasies, which enables them to better face up to them."

For Bettelheim, fairy tales have incomparable value. "They open new dimensions in the imagination of the child, which they wouldn't have discovered by themself. More importantly, the form and the structure of the fairy tales offer the child images which they can incorporate into their daydreams, helping them to better orient their life."[75]

Like a child, the Self intuitively understands the messages between the lines of these stories—a language which has no age, no time, and no nationality. For Erich Fromm, dreams and myths are all written in the same symbolic language. "The dreams of the man of Antiquity and those of the man of Modern Times are written in the same language as the myths whose authors lived at the dawn of history. It is the only universal language that humans have ever developed; it is identical across all civilizations and throughout history. This language possesses, so to speak, its grammar and its syntax and it must be understood if one shall understand the meaning of myths, fairy tales, and dreams. However, the modern Man has forgotten this language—not when he sleeps, but when he wakes."[76]

Self-transformation through rebirth

One of the recurring themes in this symbolic culture is death and life, rebirth and renewal of life. In his book *The Use of Enchantment*[77], Bruno Bettelheim identified the process of rebirth in legends and fairy tales.

In the Grimm brothers' version, after having been eaten by the big bad wolf, *Little Red Riding Hood* and her

---

[75] Bruno Bettelheim, (1976), *The Uses of Enchantment*, R. H., New York.

[76] Erich Fromm (1951), *The Forgotten Language; an introduction to the understanding of dreams, fairy tales, and myths*, 1988, R H, New York, p.16.

[77] Bruno Bettelheim (1976), *The Uses of Enchantment*, R. H., New York.

grandmother are saved by a hunter who opens the animal's stomach before filling it with stones. The message of the fairy tale is clear; if they die it is to be reborn.

Bruno Bettelheim underlines the qualitative nature of the changes that are being tell: "The rebirth that enables them to move on to a superior state is one of the leitmotifs of an immense variety of fairy tales. Children (as well as adults) must be able to believe that they can attain a superior state of existence if they master the steps of development it requires. Many adults in our time tend to take fairy tales too literally when fairy tales ought to be considered instead as the symbolic expression of the most important experiences in life. Children intuitively understand this, while also being capable of "knowing" it explicitly. The adult who tries to reassure the child by telling them that Little Red Riding Hood is not "really" dead when she is eaten by the wolf, will surely not be taken seriously. This is exactly what an adult would feel if someone told them that Jonas was not truly dead in the entrails of the whale. Anyone who understands this passage of the Bible knows intuitively that Jonas's stay in the stomach of the big fish served a specific objective: to make him come back to life in a better form."

The rebirth of Oedipus discussed in the next chapter illustrates this kind of transgenerational healing through rebirth. The hero transforms himself to become—once purified—who he really is, his true Self.

This myth illustrates that transformation involves more than merely changing oneself or altering one's beliefs and behaviors. It's about realizing one's true Self and being reborn through transgenerational integration. To heal from the consequences of a family secret, Oedipus had to let go of his old life and be reborn. This journey, symbolized by his route from Thebes to Colonus, where he ultimately became a hero and a guarantor of the city's prosperity, represents his passage through a metaphorical desert.

7
A Holistic Model

To reach a more general understanding of transgenerational integration, this chapter will present an extensive symbolic model. As we shall see, with his version of Oedipus' myth, Sophocles left us an extraordinary model of transgenerational integration, a model that allows us to articulate traditional and modern forms of transgenerational healing.

The analysis of transgenerational transmission and integration principles that I presented in the previous chapters has prepared the reader for this last stage. I started with simple case studies, progressively adding some complexity, I now invite the reader to penetrate the symbolic dimension of the psyche, closer to the unconscious and the Self. The following analysis is thus an opportunity to learn more about the symbolic language of the Self and its richness.

Sophocles' healing model also accounts for more fundamental transgenerational transmissions that are cultural and societal. These too convey faulty integrations that replay within family dynamics. Religious doctrines, societal beliefs, or cultural taboos may limit the potential for the integration of certain "unmentionable" stories, leading to unspoken truths and hidden secrets. If something is deemed immoral by a certain group during a specific era, it may lead to keeping secrets, which in turn contributes to their transgenerational transmission across generations.

These transmissions, both cultural and familial, also have some importance when it is about reconnecting with our Self. Indeed, to distinguish our true Self from what alienates us, we must consider all possible sources of alienation, not just those originating within our family.

Recognizing what differentiates one culture from another and analyzing the transition from one type of culture to another, allows us to decode possible alienations transmitted on a collective scale. That is exactly where Sophocles found himself, between two cultures, at the heart of the historic transition in Athens and at the roots of our modern civilization. That is why the discovery of a transgenerational background in Sophocles' work on Oedipus is a major discovery. By putting in writing wisdom that had previously been transmitted orally, Sophocles conveyed ancestral knowledge for generations to come. Like a great-uncle or a grandmother would pass down a family history, Sophocles fulfilled the same function on a cultural scale.

Sophocles as a traditional therapist

The great tragedians of Ancient Greece, like Sophocles, assumed the invaluable function to guide the collective consciousness. They included ancient traditions (some initiatory) in their plays, performed in huge amphitheaters where the whole community would gather. They dealt with events and problems (moral, religious, political, and military) that preoccupied the minds of their fellow citizens. Somehow, Greek tragedies were a way of modernizing ancient rites and other collective ceremonies that were becoming more and more secular.

Every year, tragedians were judged on the quality of their plays and the relevance of their messages. Sophocles was recognized as a genius and was crowned 18 to 23 times, otherwise finishing second. He was also appointed to fulfill important functions, as the administrator of the treasure of Delos, General, or Councillor in charge of the city. Sophocles was the friend of many other great minds that flourished in that unique moment of history. Together they would give birth to a new, more democratic, ideal of what civilization should look like.

Sophocles was a modern man in his time while remaining respectful of ancient traditions, particularly those that fulfilled a therapeutic function. The countless analyses of his plays that exist fail to sufficiently highlight that Sophocles belonged to a tradition of scholars and initiates who combined the performing arts, healing, spirituality, and religion. This comprehensive vision has been lost with the compartmentalization of academic disciplines. This fragmentation of knowledge prevents Hellenists and scholars from truly grasping the psychological and therapeutic significance of Sophocles' plays. Likewise, apart from depth psychologists, modern psychologists and psychiatrists ignore the tremendous therapeutic potential in these ancient forms of wisdom.

How could academic studies dissociate Sophocles from the traditional therapeutic culture he was a part of? His father and his family held the title of priesthood of Amynos, the healing god. Pierre Vidal-Naquet explains that Sophocles was a "pious man, a member of a group who worshipped the hero-doctor Amynos (the Helpful)."[78] When synthesizing his multiple qualities, it is possible to view Sophocles as a psycho-shaman[79], a mediator between

---

[78] Pierre Vidal-Naquet (1994) « Œdipe à Athènes », dans *Œdipe et ses mythes*, avec Jean-Pierre Vernant, Complexe, Paris.

[79] See my article: « Sophocles, Psycho-shamanic Ancestor », in *Shamanism, Ancestors and Transgenerational Integration*, collective book, Genesis Editions, Geneva.

worlds—bridging the traditional and the modern, the visible and the invisible.

A hidden teaching

In Athens, under the pretext of "realism", there was an increasing tendency to view the world by its mere appearances. Because of their religious references, symbolic forms of discourse (poems, myths, etc.) were replaced by other forms favoring reason and rationality. Nietzsche and many others emphasized how humanity lost a part of its essence during this civilizational shift. Today, the repression and the loss of a more symbolic relationship to the world hinder our potential, making it difficult to go beyond appearances, where the true meaning of our life experiences lies.

Sophocles' teachings are not easy to recognize, especially today when the importance of transgenerational heritages has largely been forgotten. Just like with traditional initiations, his teachings are not explicitly stated. They are kept for those who can discover a hidden message between the lines of a hermeneutic narrative—a message presented in an obvious way to those able to see without filters. This requires moving beyond the confines of rational thought to access a more symbolic message. This is a real challenge—much like any initiation—because readers and spectators of the Oedipus myth must also confront their unconscious resistance. The more modern culture alienates them, the stronger this resistance becomes, thus further distancing them from the myth's true meaning.

Indeed, we must go beyond appearances and the taboos on incest and parricide to see that Oedipus' story[80]

---

[80] Summaries of *Oedipus the King* and *Oedipus at Colonus* will be found in the annex.

reflects the different stages of transgenerational integration work. It is a myth that recounts the transformation of a symptom (the plague described at the beginning of *Oedipus the King*) into a blessing (the prosperity found at the end of *Oedipus at Colonus*).

Sophocles' play recounts how Oedipus discovers the true identity of his parents. This revelation allows him to integrate his tragedy and everything that occurred earlier in his life when he was alienated by the secret of his birth—having been secretly adopted. In the second play, *Oedipus at Colonus*, Sophocles describes how Oedipus transforms into his true Self, becoming the hero of Colonus and guaranteeing prosperity for all.

Until today, none of the interpretations of Oedipus' fate have made any reference to the transgenerational thread that can be found throughout the play. While these themes may seem apparent, they might have been missed because modern culture has largely forgotten about transgenerational principles. Sophocles, on the other hand, belonged to a community that was well aware of the problems that transgenerational heritages could cause. As I discussed in Chapter Two, they first addressed these issues by invoking divine will and then sought to liberate themselves from its burdens.

A metaphorical language

The symbolic language that characterizes mythology (its *Mythos)* lends itself to numerous analogies. For example, the fall and rebirth at the core of the myth of Oedipus can be likened to the dramatic rises and falls experienced by contemporary celebrities, who often undergo a period of personal crisis before emerging renewed or reinvented. This metaphor also captures the universal highs and lows of life that no one is spared from.

One must also understand the relationship between the kingdom and its king, as a metaphor for what is played out between the body and its spirit. Symbolically, Oedipus, as the King of Thebes, is the head of the kingdom (as if the kingdom represented his own body). Oedipus' quest to eradicate the plague from further ravaging his kingdom is comparable to that of a sick man battling an illness, like cancer or depression.

In addition, the central theme in Sophocles' work: prosperity, relates to the worship of Demeter, the goddess of agriculture and harvest, who is worshipped at Eleusis, near Athens. The cycle of the seasons and the harvests provide a model based on fertility and rebirths. This theme stands at the core of the *Eleusinian Mysteries* initiations. Within this matriarchal context (one that was not aware of the link between sexuality and birth and was thus deprived of the representation of a "father"), an Oedipal theme already existed, that of a son of the goddess, who with each new season had to fertilize his Mother Earth to ensure the renewal of life. Under this ancient matriarchal regime, divine incest was "natural," since the reproductive role of men's sexuality had not been understood. Consequently, the symbolic dimension of fatherhood did not exist.

Sophocles' masterpiece on Oedipus addresses all these themes. It begins with a terrible plague that ravages agriculture, animals, and humans[81]. However, at the end of Oedipus' journey, the curtain falls with the promise of prosperity. Between these two extremes, Sophocles talks of Oedipus' transformation, an effective rebirth.

Finally, the themes of parricide and incest should not be reduced as merely horrible behavior or taken as literal

[81] With the increasing utilization of natural resources, pollution and the epidemic of certain illnesses, we are still, if not more than ever, concerned by this teaching.

events. Doing so would mean staying prisoner of appearances[82]. Instead, we must remember to respect the symbolic dimension of the myth. There is a teaching awaiting those who manage to go beyond this first mental trap.

Once we overcome this tendency to misjudge the story, we can recognize it as a metaphoric return to Mother Earth, and as a ritual transition from childhood to adulthood—a theme central to many traditional cultures. Freud's focus on the transgression of taboos reduces and sensationalizes the myth of Oedipus, in a typically modern way. His analysis, in this sense, falls into the trap set by traditional teaching. True understanding of Sophocles' message is achieved only by bypassing these pitfalls and respecting the myth's symbolic nature. As we shall see, the return to Mother Earth is represented in the myth by his reunion with Jocasta. Because he was alienated at birth, Oedipus needed to meet Jocasta in order to discover the secret of his origins that had until then prevented him from becoming his true Self. In essence, from the perspective of Sophocles, Oedipus has not yet been truly born, and the discovery of his "incestuous" position, or symbiotic state, is the starting point for the birth of his true Self.

Restoring lost prosperity

Let us now look at how Sophocles used these transgenerational laws to write the myth of Oedipus, considered to be one of the greatest masterpieces of antiquity.

By presenting Oedipus as a victim of the secret of his biological parents' true identities, Sophocles demonstrates the possible tragic consequences of such a family secret. Through incest and parricide, the myth illustrates the

---

82 This confusion can be compared with a person who would call the police when she sees actors playing a bank robbery, unable to understand that it is not a real crime, but it's representation, that is being played out

worst things that can happen when we do not respect the passing on of truths in families. However, if Sophocles “paints the devil on the wall”, it is mainly to provide us with a magisterial teaching, which is that one can turn the worst of tragedies into a potential for personal development and transformation. Indeed, his teaching is essentially that of a healing model, as it ends with the guarantee of restored prosperity.

In his version of Oedipus' myth, Sophocles plays on two levels of consciousness. What looks like a tragedy on a first level of consciousness, turns out to be therapeutic release on another. To move from one level of consciousness to the next, it is important to know about transgenerational principles and be aware of the concept of *ate*—a term referring to a transgenerational curse or a fate of ill reputation among the Ancient Greeks. From this perspective, we can see how revealing a secret about his true parentage can turn tragedy into a liberating catharsis. By reconnecting with his origins—through the discovery of his biological parents' true identities—Oedipus was able to integrate this initially alienated part of his life, of which he'd been unaware. The transformation of the plague (at the beginning of *Oedipus the King*) into prosperity (at the end of *Oedipus at Colonus*) also accounts for Sophocles' therapeutic purpose—Oedipus' healing coincides with the healing of the entire community.

From alienation to the birth of the Self

There are many ways[83] in which we could bring to light the transgenerational thread that underlies Sophocles' work. To sum up, I suggest looking at the significant steps of Oedipus' journey from Thebes to Colonus. We may already highlight two periods: Oedipus' first life as king of

[83] For a more extensive transgenerational analysis and discussion, *A Model for Healing Family Curses*, Genesis Editions (2024)

Thebes (when he was not aware of the identity of his parents), and his second life in which he integrates his true origins to really become himself.

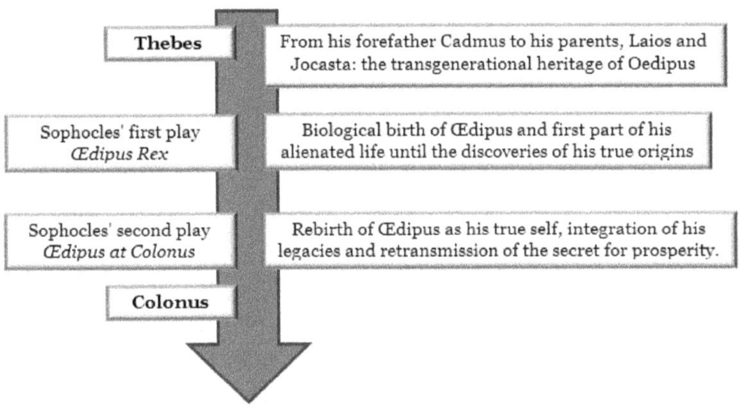

The plague of Thebes

At the beginning of the play, the plague represents the symptom that motivates the quest of the future hero. Sophocles describes the ravaged situation: "Death strikes in the germs where fruits are formed from its soil, death strikes in its herds of oxen, in its women, who no longer give life." Just like a client who comes in to talk about a problem he wants to solve, Oedipus wants to save his Kingdom from the plague, "at whatever cost!" Sophocles' work begins with a scenario akin to a consultation where one seeks to understand, resolve, and heal a troubling situation.

In response to that sort of demand, Sophocles' answer is given indirectly through Tiresias's prediction: "This day will see your birth and your death all at once." Here as well, we can draw a parallel with a work on the unconscious reality, and how once it has been integrated, it can lead to profound change. Depth Psychology shares with these ancient initiations the idea of a fundamental transformation of the person. Depth Psychology, like Sophocles, also recognizes that symptoms have a mission to awaken the unconscious Self. Instead of seeking to superficially eliminate these symptoms, it sees them as a motor and a compass to better understand one's Self.

Unfinished mourning causes the plague

Just as we consult specialists of the unconscious today, people in ancient times sought the guidance of oracles or seers. When asked how to save the city from the plague, Tiresias explained to Oedipus that the Thebans needed to uncover the circumstances surrounding the death of the previous king, Laius, and identify his murderer. At the heart of the problem lies the association between the unfinished mourning caused by the mysterious disappearance of Laius, and the non-renewal of life (the plague). In other words, as long as these circumstances are not clarified, successful mourning cannot take place, thus blocking the cycle of life. Such are the consequences of disrespecting an ancient law of granting funerals to the dead so that peace can reign among the living. Here again, the oracle represents the approach that a transgenerational analyst might have, which is to decipher the possible presence of incomplete mourning, as this may be at the heart of such symptoms.

The play *Oedipus the King* recounts the evolution of Oedipus' investigation into the circumstances of Laius's death. Oedipus must clarify what happened prior to his arrival in Thebes. Similarly, in modern transgenerational analysis, one often needs to uncover a hidden history that continues to weigh heavily on the present. Oedipus' quest leads him to discover that Polybius and Merope, King and Queen of Corinth, are not his real parents. Suffering from infertility, Polybius and Merope had secretly decided to adopt him after a shepherd found him on Mount Cithaeron.

Oedipus' search for the truth regarding the death of the former King of Thebes reveals other startling truths. The testimony of an escaped servant, along with his memories, forces Oedipus to recognize that he's the one who killed Laius in self-defense. Before he arrived in Thebes, a stranger had provoked him leading to a fatal struggle in which Oedipus emerged victorious, unknowingly killing his own father. However, the worst discovery was yet to come. This same servant explains that Laius and Jocasta were his parents and that they had decided three days after his birth to abandon him on Mount Cithaeron, where he was left hanging by his feet for the wild beasts. It was there that a shepherd from Corinth had saved him and brought him to Polybius and Merope, who had then adopted him.

This quest mirrors what a client might go through when clarifying their family tree/history. The myth also tells us of certain resistances we may encounter and which we must overcome to uncover the truth, as when Jocasta tries to dissuade Oedipus from continuing his quest.

Along with secrets and their impact on the individual, transgenerational analysis can also shed light on the hidden identity of a family member such as a supposed brother. It thus explains pathological family dynamics. Incomplete bereavements are also often found, providing some understanding as to why some parents were unable to offer tenderness and affection to their children. Finally, even when we think we have discovered an unfinished story in our ancestors, it can be the consequence of an older story.

Pentheus' unintegrated story

Besides the consequences of Laius' unfinished mourning, there are more tragedies to be found in the history of the Labdacids—Oedipus' family. Another tragic destiny that we need to consider is that of King Pentheus, who was the first to succeed Cadmus, the founder of Thebes. Pentheus is the great-grandfather of Oedipus.

Pentheus' death is tragic because he was killed by his own mother as she was celebrating the famous bacchanals on Mount Cithaeron. While in a trance, she thought she had seen a lion and threw herself onto him to tear him apart with her bare hands. When she recovered her senses, she discovered what she had done, and the poor woman was inconsolable. This traumatic infanticide was never integrated by the Thebans. That is why Oedipus nearly suffered the same fate when his parents decided to hang him by his feet on the same Mount Cithaeron. The act of infanticide was almost repeated in the same place! However, Oedipus miraculously survived, foreshadowing that he would survive all the tribulations on his path to becoming a hero.

The two lineages of Cadmus

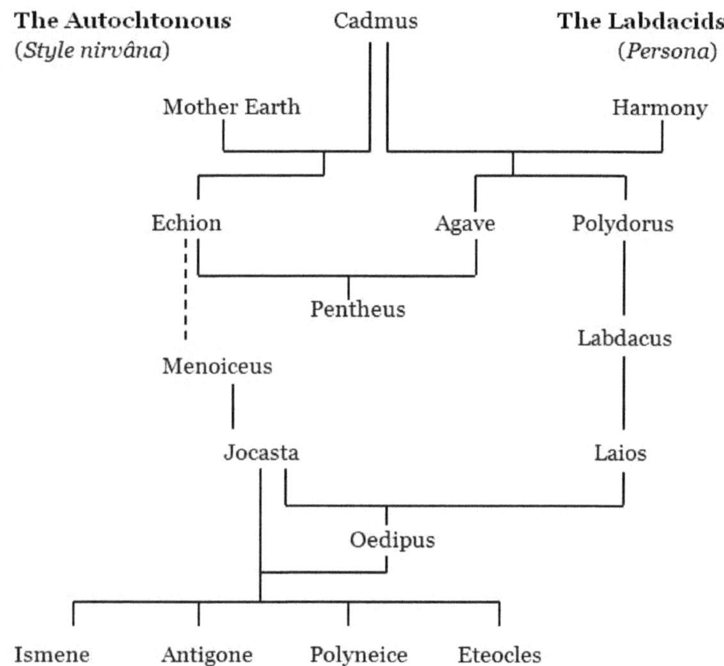

All of Cadmus's descendants were alienated by the women's inability to mourn Pentheus' death. This heritage culminates with the tragic story of Antigone. The unfinished mourning found among women of this matrilineal line affects the ability of their sons to mourn the deaths of their fathers. Indeed, there is a recurring problem in the Labdacids lineage, the patrilineage line: all the fathers have died prematurely, making it impossible for their sons to mourn their passing properly. Didier Dumas analyzes this generational pattern until Laius, noting that, "his childhood, like that of the young Louis XIV, was marked by bloody struggles over the succession which obliged him to flee Thebes."

The history of his paternal lineage for the three generations preceding Laius was marked by the tragic deaths of the fathers. His father, King Labdacos (the "Lame"), died when he was still a child. Labdacos himself was his father's orphan."[84] These incomplete bereavements across generations produced a new symptom—Laius's infertility. Only the prediction of a patricidal son could counterbalance his sterility, much to his own misfortune. Given these details, we can better understand the nature of the lack of integration inherited by Oedipus, even before he was conceived.

The transferential needs of Jocasta and Laius

The lack of integration of Agave's infanticide, on the side of Jocasta, and the undone griefs of the fathers, on the side of Laius, are responsible for the couple's sterility. The oracle they interrogate dissuades them from having a child, as said child would be parricidal and incestuous if they were born. But neither Jocasta nor Laius understands the oracle's message as an invitation to undertake introspective work and discover the origin of their sterility—

[84] Didier Dumas (2000), *Et l'enfant créa le père*, Hachette Littérature, Paris.

their transgenerational alienations. Instead, like the *Personae*, they are content to project the oracle's prediction onto their future child, placing the burden of unresolved transgenerational legacies from both lineages on him before he's even born. If they are no longer sterile when they conceive Oedipus, it is because they have passed on their unintegrated issues to him. Everything is set to repeat Pentheus' tragedy. Like his illustrious forefather, Oedipus will be the victim of an infanticide attempt in the same place, on Mount Cithaeron. A few generations later, the story repeats itself, with the difference that Oedipus will be saved by a shepherd from Corinth.

This transmission of the lack of integrations of Laius and Jocasta informs us about the nature of the transgenerational alienations Oedipus inherited even before being conceived.

Oedipus explains, "What could I do? All was foretold by the gods, and it was they who brought it all to pass. It was they who ordained that I should do these things, and I did them, all unknowing, in the madness of my fate. [...] Ah, if only I had never been born! I would have been better off not to have been conceived at all, but I was born—though why my parents, knowing the oracle's prophecy, allowed me to be born, I do not understand"

As I develop it in my other books, it is no coincidence that *Oedipus the King* begins with the plague that renders the entire kingdom sterile. For Oedipus, this is a mirror of Laius and Jocasta's sterility that he will have to integrate to be born as his true Self—and to no longer be a victim of the lack of integration accumulated in his two parental lines.

Another aspect to consider is how symptoms are passed down through the Labdacids' lineage. Because Oedipus's feet were swollen from being bound, he was given a name that means "swollen feet" in Greek. This theme of foot problems appears again in his ancestors: Labdacos was lame, and Laius was described as "awkward and clumsy, struggling to maintain his balance." These symptoms evoke a painful relationship with Mother Earth, who, in this family, suffers from the inability to integrate Agave's infanticide.

It is also important to briefly mention another tragedy that created another ghost, this time relating to Laius. He had abused his host's son, Chrysippus, who had afterward committed suicide. Chrysippus's father, King Pelops, then cast a curse (*ate*) onto Laius. According to some analysts, it is for this reason that Laius was condemned to perish at the hands of his son.

The Labdacids lineage

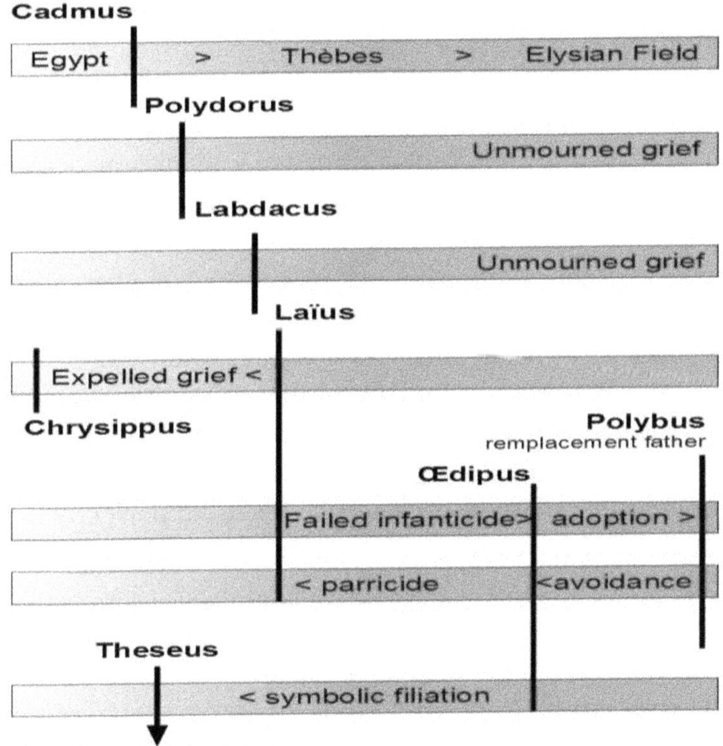

Jocasta's and Laius's debts

These unfinished stories are all inherited by Oedipus at birth. From Jocasta, he inherited the impact of Agave's infanticide and the incomplete bereavement of Pentheus, a heritage that extends to Antigone. Through his father, Oedipus inherited a series of unresolved issues: the strained relationships between fathers and sons, the unfinished mourning of fathers by their sons, a recurring problem with feet (and a connection to Mother Earth), and a curse that befell his father Laius due to his wrongful actions.

This heritage is even more unconscious, in that Oedipus was the victim of a secret regarding the true identity of his parents. Deprived of any possibility to integrate his transgenerational heritage, Oedipus unconsciously reenacts these unintegrated stories in typical *nirvana style* fashion: he kills a father who had first tried to kill him, and he marries a mother who had abandoned him at birth. His first life leads him to replay what had unconsciously alienated him, turning it against those responsible for his situation. Sophocles' portrayal of Oedipus's parricidal and incestuous fate exemplifies my definition of *nirvana style* that unconsciously replays the causes of transgenerational alienation. Oedipus' nirvana style responds here to the *Personas* of Laius and Jocasta, who were both unable to integrate their transgenerational heritages (which manifested in the form of the sterility of the couple), therefore, transmitting them to their sons. This myth perfectly illustrates the functioning of unconscious transgenerational transmissions.

It is only by discovering his parricide and incest that Oedipus unveils the origins of his unconscious alienation: the secret of his birth and adoption. In parallel to this crisis, another process can thus take place; a process that will lead to his rebirth, or the birth of his true Self.

A life-changing truth

Thanks to the revelation of Oedipus' true origins, two realities overlapped. On the one hand, Oedipus had unwittingly transgressed taboos on parricide and incest. Despite his lack of intent, he is still considered guilty of these offenses, which is why he chose to blind himself. He questioned the value of his eyes, lamenting that despite his good intentions, he had been deceived by appearances.

On the other hand, Oedipus has become aware of his real origins. Despite the tragedy, and even thanks to it, he discovered a secret that had alienated him, making him an unconscious victim since birth. The tragedy allowed him to reconnect with his origins and integrate them, this second reality slowly taking precedence over the first. His newfound awareness allowed him to integrate his history. By recognizing his transgenerational heritage and the unfinished stories of his ancestors, he could finally come to terms with them. As long as he was alienated by the secret of his origins, he couldn't become his true self. A similar process occurs when transgenerational analysis reveals hidden stories in a family history. Although disillusionment may occur, such as during "teenage crises", it is a necessary step towards gaining more consciousness and becoming one's real Self.

For Oedipus, this stepping stone symbolizes a form of rebirth, infusing his transgression of taboos with a new meaning. From then on, he could differentiate the first part of his life from the second part after he discovered who he truly was. As the many therapeutic examples have shown, when a person discovers they are the victim of a family secret, they can understand their story from a completely different angle. This new perspective allows the individual to reconsider old relationships and events, to make peace with their history, to integrate it, and to start afresh on a new and more solid foundation.

A process of rebirth

In his second play, *Oedipus at Colonus*, Sophocles puts integration work into action. Faced with what might be considered the most dramatic situation imaginable for a man, Oedipus can from then, rely on his newly acquired awareness. This allows him to re-establish the relationship with his true Self, which until then was perverted by secrets unknown to him. With this new awareness comes the ability to integrate a story that would have seemed impossible to overcome otherwise. Again, Sophocles gifts us with an important teaching: as soon as the truth becomes conscious, it enables us to integrate what previously appeared to be an impasse. Because it broadens our consciousness, access to the truth permits the integration of a situation that seemed impossible to resolve. Such consciousness allows the true Self to arise with unexpectedly resilient potential. This teaching is, in every respect, similar to Pindar's famous words, "learn what you are, and be such."

The benefits of integration work

In *Oedipus at Colonus*, Sophocles recounts how Oedipus obtains Theseus's hospitality, allowing him to reconnect with the community. Here, Sophocles highlights the significance of Theseus's attitude, as he recognizes the true self in Oedipus, looking beyond his tarnished reputation. Theseus perceives a fundamental humanity in Oedipus that resonates with his own. Having experienced exile himself, Theseus understands that the future is unpredictable. His noble attitude reflects the ideals of the emerging civilization in Athens. Sophocles offers a profound lesson through Theseus's attitude toward Oedipus: a hermeneutist who sees beyond surface judgments to recognize the essence of another. This recognition provides therapeutic benefits for Oedipus.

From the moment Theseus offers his hospitality to Oedipus, the story plays out as a countdown. The theme of parental rejection, repeated with his expulsion from Thebes, gives way to social reintegration. It is impossible not to see the parallel with certain rites of passage, where children must pass through caves in the dark (or through Mother Earth/Jocasta) before being reintegrated into the community[85] as adults.

In return for Theseus's generous hospitality, Oedipus promises he will entrust him with a secret that will ensure his people's prosperity. This promise represents the culmination of Oedipus's efforts to integrate his transgenerational legacies, marking the end of his tragic cycle. By surviving his alienations and their associated trials and tribulations, Oedipus is able to transform these alienations into something positive (symptoms into symbols). The message he entrusts to Theseus is the opposite of the one he had received from his parents. However, as the story concludes: the people must not forget Oedipus, or they risk losing the assurance of their future prosperity. This demonstrates Sophocles' adherence to the ancient forms of ancestor worship, whose celebrations were believed to ensure the prosperity of the descendants.

The return to grace

Although formerly a victim of his transgenerational alienations, Oedipus was able to integrate them, therefore regaining the favor of the Gods. Ismene states, "The gods, who have destroyed you, now raise you up again." Pierre Vidal-Naquet emphasizes the significance of this reversal in Sophocles' writing: "In both Philoctetes and Oedipus at

---

[85] For the complete analysis, see (2024), *A Model for Healing Family Curses, Oedipus' journey from outcast to hero of Colonus, Genesis Editions, Geneva.*

Colonus, Sophocles depicts not just separation but also return. Even as he presents the old exiles becoming heroes, separation remains a necessary stage."

Oedipus explains that "when I am nothing then I am a man."[86] Another translation even says: "It is at that point, when I am nothing, that I am really myself."[87]

To be "nothing" here means to relinquish the roles and masks one adopts, representing a *persona* that the individual puts on to deal with alienation. Only then can the true self emerge. This idea resonates with many ancient traditions and modern practices, including therapy and personal development. The restoration of grace from the gods symbolizes reconnecting with one's divine origins, a concept central to all traditional cultures. After all, are we not like the leaves of a tree, rooted in the Earth and spreading out to the sky, connected to our origins?

Overall perspective

Because the Thebans were unable to grieve the first infanticide of their history, they projected Pentheus' onto Oedipus. They, later, restored him to the throne without knowing his true identity or origins. Once his real identity was revealed, Oedipus could no longer be mistaken for Pentheus. He lost his replacement role and became a scapegoat for the community's unresolved issues. Thus, in Oedipus at Colonus, even though the Thebans seek to reclaim the blessings of their former king, they are not worthy of them until they complete their mourning for Pentheus. In contrast, the Athenians who offered him hospitality—Colonus being a close village of Athens—deserve the secret that will ensure their prosperity.

---

[86] Sophocles, *The Three Theban Plays*, translated by Robert Fagles, Penguin Classics, 1982, New York, p. 306.

[87] David Green's translation, *Sophocles I: Antigone, Oedipus the King, Oedipus at Colonus* University of Chicago Press (2013)

This analysis shows that Oedipus had to emancipate himself from the scapegoat role projected onto him by the community. This projection was grounded in a transferential need, addressing their unresolved grief over Pentheus's death. Therefore, Sophocles' model is richer in teachings than simple examples of family therapy. In addition to his transgenerational family heritage, Oedipus needed to transition from the Thebans to the Athenians to complete his integration journey. This allowed him to reconnect with his origins, or in other words, to regain the gods' grace.

Oedipus' integration of his origins

The prosperity
The plague
The roots
Labdacides lineage
Theseus
Prosperous legacy
Integration and emancipations
Fall, rebirth and exil
Laius
Œdipus
Jocasta
Labdacus
Polydorus
Harmonia
Cadmus
The Mother Earth
Echion
Pentheus
Native lineage
Œdipus at Colunus
Œdipus Rex

Through his representation of the plague, Sophocles underlines the repercussions that a king will have on a city if he is alienated by his transgenerational heritages and ignores his origins. Traditionally, the king was responsible for the proper functioning of his kingdom. A just and legitimate rule, aligned with the gods and the land, would ensure the city's future. Conversely, any dysfunction would be felt by the community which would then turn against the king. This relationship between the responsibility of the king and the prosperity of his kingdom is not just a Greek concept. It also existed in Ancient Egypt, where the Pharaoh had to respect the invisible laws of life to provide a good balance for their land. By contrasting the plague with the promise of prosperity, Sophocles emphasizes the importance of a living relationship with one's origins, free from self-ignorance, thereby concluding his final play.

Family tree healing brings prosperity

In Sophocles' time, this hermeneutical[88] tradition was represented by Asclepius, the God of healing, whose sanctuary at Epidaurus was renowned for its cures and healings. Archaeological findings suggest that Sophocles himself was a priest for Asclepius. This would explain why he had the honor to house the statue of Asclepius while waiting for the god's temple to be achieved in Athens. Considering the importance of these traditional practices, it is surprising to see that Sophocles' roots in therapeutic traditions have not been accounted for in former analyses.

My research on the transgenerational structure underlying Oedipus' myth has only brought me closer to this important tradition. It should be noted that many other schools of thought are also indebted to hermeticism. While psychoanalysis considers the unconscious, many other approaches still do not take this reality into account. Psychoanalysis is, however, guilty of not giving enough attention to previous psychological knowledge and ancient wisdom. This also explains why psychoanalysis remains

[88] A lineage that starts with Thot-Hermès, continues with Hermes Trismegistus, Asclepius and Sophocles.

dependent on a modern culture that has forgotten the transgenerational laws. It was, therefore, time to re-interpret Oedipus' myth in depth, rather than widen the gap that separates the modern and the ancient world. This allows us to re-establish the link between modern and ancient knowledge, enabling them to be renewed in a broader sense, that of Depth Psychology.

Faithful to ancient teachings, the guarantee of prosperity that Oedipus leaves to Theseus is similar to the restoration of the fertile unity of the origins. Integrating transgenerational heritage allows the individual to reconnect with a fertile source, which is observable in the transformation of the plague into a symbolic fertility.

From symptom to symbol

Oedipus' journey illustrates very well this transformation of symptoms into symbols which I have already mentioned several times. In fact, integration is situated between two poles. On one side there is a given situation that is seen as problematic and from which questions arise (in the myth: the plague), and on the other side, there is its symbolization, synonymous with something that has been learned and can be transmitted (the guarantee of prosperity). Between these two poles is a workspace; a space in which personal development can take place. This space allows the Self to grow, the person to integrate their life events, to rewrite their story, and to root it in the present day.

This perspective matches the etymological definitions of "symptom" and "symbol." These terms are composed of two parts. The first part "sym" is identical, and the second part differentiates the two terms. The first part refers to the action of bringing objects and events together (*sum*). The second part refers to two different ways of bringing things together. The "ptom" of symptom comes from "pipto," an involuntary action; whereas "ballo," in symbol, refers to a voluntary action. For example, a symptom in the form of a phobia of mice associates the sight of the little animal with a sensation of fear. It is an involuntary association, that is to say, it is symptomatic.

By contrast, elements that are put together voluntarily give the symbol its overall message. The ability to work easily with the parts of a whole, bringing them together or separating them, is a sign of an operative symbol. An example would be the pendants in the form of two half-hearts that lovers share, and which like other objects from the time of our ancestors, designate the bonds that join two people, two families, or two clans. The Tao, which represents the union of "Yin" and "Yang", is the symbol of the fertile and creative transcendence of an encounter between the masculine and the feminine; it depicts the unity of complementary poles.

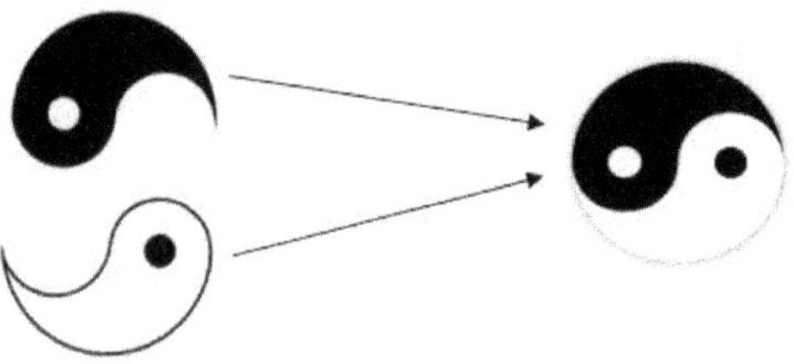

In sharp contrast to the work of integration, it is interesting to comment on the word "diabolic," because it designates the voluntary action of disassociating joint elements. In contrast to "sum," which signifies gathering, "dia" signifies a dividing; posing an obstacle to a union and separating the components concerned. Secrets, unsaid things, and other distortions or manipulations of reality are quite literally "diabolical" actions—sometimes used unconsciously, sometimes deliberately and perversely. Integration work seeks to overcome these actions. For Didier Dumas, as you might recall, the absence of open communication on historical events, or traumas, is the source of transgenerational alienations. These absences of speech and the lack of symbolization work against a unifying function and alienate future generations. The "guilty parties" are those who refuse to speak or open their hearts, and who instead foster a lack of integration—a "past that is not past"—passing it on to those closest to them. They disassociate their feelings (repressed or denied) from the discourse that should be used to accompany[89] and authenticity that characterizes neurotic relationships, and in more serious cases, perverse relationships.

Coming back to the Self

Sophocles' model demonstrates that transgenerational analysis also concerns the true Self, which, despite its alienations, seeks to emerge.

Therefore, we find ourselves in the presence of two complementary movements. On one hand, there is the work of updating our unconscious heritages which can be undertaken with family tree analysis. On the other hand, we can know ourselves better with the analysis of our unconscious parts and our "dark sides." Together, these two efforts allow us to integrate our symbolic (rather than historical) origins and our true Self. If we consider that the Gods are at the origin of all things in traditional culture, then when Oedipus finds the grace of the Gods, this means that he has reconnected with himself and with the source—a fertile unity.

Sophocles' depiction of the journey from Thebes to Colonus reflects an inner, initiatory journey, which leads the hero back to his true Self. The person Oedipus was looking for at the very beginning of his quest, turned out to be none other than himself. Though its presentation is somewhat ironic, the message it conveys is profoundly

---

[89] All spiritual traditions cultivate this coherence between thought, word and deed, a guarantee of harmony and wisdom.

wise. It reminds us how much we are a part of this world, and that the supposed gap between the outside and the inside might be nothing more than an illusion. The knowledge we seek is not something to be found at the end of a journey, it has been within us from the very beginning.

Even if we are not aware of it, the Self within us is constantly present. In the present moment, we can become true to ourselves. Eckhart Tollé[90] compares a man wondering about the nature of the present moment to a fish worrying that it cannot become aware of the water it swims in. This relation to one's Self is inherent, but we forget it the moment we become estranged from ourselves—when we are alienated. An ancient legend captures this situation perfectly: To punish Men for their abuses, the Gods decided to hide their share of divinity where they would never think to look—deep within themselves.

---

[90] Eckhart Tolle (2004), *The Power of Now*, Namaste Publishing, Vancouver.

8
Become Who You Are

As I explained in the introduction, we are not just the result of our past, nor the simple fruit of our family tree. It would be too limiting to define a person by their biological and psychological heritage, even though they may have an important impact on our lives, as the therapeutic examples have shown.

As we have seen, transgenerational heritages perpetuate the unintegrated stories of our ancestors. However, this dependence on past events is relative; it depends on whether we have a passive or active attitude. As Sophocles' model shows, the active quest for the meaning behind our symptoms can help decipher family secrets and the transgenerational inheritances that have alienated us. The discovery of the truth can certainly be difficult. Nevertheless, it can be a necessary step towards reconnecting with new resources and integrating our heritages from the perspective of the true Self. Like Oedipus, becoming who we truly are is a process that can turn tragedies into opportunities for healing.

With Oedipus, Sophocles illustrates the famous saying of Pindar, a Greek poet of the 5th century B.C. "Become who you are, having learned what that is." In those days, to know one's genealogy and to discover who you were in relation to your origins was a must. This process required an active participation, where one had to reclaim their family history. As Goethe put it, what we have received from our ancestors, we must assimilate until it becomes a part of ourselves if we want to turn it into an enrichment rather than a burden. As we have discussed, it is the Self in us that can integrate its heritages and origins while developing at the same time. In doing so, it becomes what it has always been, without knowing it until that instant. Oedipus after having found inner peace, says: "It is when I am nothing that I am truly myself."

The Hermeneutics of the Self

What does it take for the Self to develop? Here again, Sophocles offers us clues: it is Theseus's hospitality towards Oedipus that makes the difference. Theseus takes on the role of a therapist, showing empathy toward the true Self that he recognizes in Oedipus. If Oedipus, former King of Thebes, finds hospitality in a new land, it is because Sophocles wanted to show us the benefits that a city can reap from welcoming another person as their true Self. For this to happen, the city, or its king, like Theseus, must be able to recognize the true self in the person asking for hospitality, and provide the condition for that true self to emerge. An attitude which reflects that Athenian citizen are also longing to become their true Selves. Like their king, they want to be capable of thinking for themselves and exercising their new democratic rights—unlike in Thebes, where the citizens failed to do so and therefore to solve the Sphinx's riddle.

Thanks to Theseus' welcome, Oedipus can finish integrating his history and regain the grace of the Gods. Armed with new, hard-won knowledge, Oedipus can now pass down a positive legacy to those who deserve it.

In Sophocles' model, Theseus is an essential character. Despite his horrible reputation, Theseus recognizes the

Self in Oedipus. Thus, he fulfills the role of a hermeneutist[91], one who can see beyond appearances and allow the true Self to develop.

Behind appearances: everything is already present

The hermeneutist can interpret appearances, as did Tiresias who, at the beginning of *Oedipus the King*, sees the meaning and origins of the plague. He can access the hidden meaning behind the symptoms.

In therapy, it is also important to recognize what lies behind first impressions. Here is a new example of transgenerational analysis, one that illustrates how present-day difficulties can reflect unconscious issues. Catherine divorced due to her ex- husband's behavior, including his dependence on paid sexual services. In parallel, she began therapy to understand the unconscious conflicts replaying in her marriage. While we were analyzing the unfinished stories of her ancestors, we made certain discoveries that gave new meaning to the trials she had experienced.

To begin with, she realized that she had adopted the role of a mother, attempting to repair what had been lacking in her ancestors' lives, particularly with respect to her grandfather, whose mother had left home when he was just a child. This grandfather had then led a double life, being in an open relationship with another woman while remaining married. He left his marital home to his wife but provided another house to his mistress, stipulating that this house should eventually be passed down to his descendants—Catherine's mother, and then to Catherine herself.

Having never previously thought about the importance of her inheritance, Catherine began to question

---

[91] Hermeneutics is an art of interpreting signs and to reach deeper meanings beyond appearances.

herself further, particularly as she felt wronged in the division of the family home during her divorce. For the first time, in order to explore these questions of money and inheritance, she asked her mother about them. Catherine was surprised to discover that her mother had squandered most of the money from the sale of the house, and of several other family estates that had once belonged to her grandmother, the wife of the aforementioned grandfather. In addition, Catherine became fully aware of her mother's complete lack of interest in passing on the family legacy that Catherine's grandfather had intended for her.

Catherine could now better understand why she felt so cheated by her ex-husband. The betrayal had begun long before the divorce, with a mother who did not intend to follow her father's wishes and pass on the inheritance to her daughter. Catherine was, in fact, deprived of the family legacy her grandfather wanted her to have.She then made other, even more startling, discoveries. As she recalled some past conversations with third parties, Catherine realized that her mother had also paid for sexual services—just like her ex-husband. With the money that had been wasted on their sexual addiction, and the fact that she had been cheated financially, Catherine saw these two aspects of her experience as reflective of each other. The parallel stories of her mother and her ex-husband acted as two mirrors, reflecting the same underlying issues. What she had endured with her ex-husband illuminated the reality of her relationship with her mother.

Of course, this is a classic theme in psychoanalysis, where unresolved issues in the relationship with one's parents are replayed in the couple's dynamic. However, in this case, it was necessary to trace back through several generations to fully understand Catherine's unconscious issues and recognize that her husband was replaying these dynamics right before her eyes, in a sort of "nirvana style" reenactment. From there, she was able to re-assess her own story as well as those played out by her ancestors and live out her relationship with her mother from a new standpoint; with greater awareness which prevented her from repeating similar patterns in the future.

This example shows how the transgenerational legacies of our ancestors' repressed events are replayed in our lives, even if they escape our consciousness, "everything is there".

To delve into what is

Integration work takes inspiration from a specific approach called phenomenology,[92] which is focused on the present moment, the "here and now" of our life experiences. This attention given to the present that enables us to reach the Self is found in many Oriental spiritual teachings.

In our Western culture, a similar approach to the present moment also exists: phenomenology. Formulas such as, *I feel, therefore I am* or *Here and now*, which emerged as a reaction against the dualistic mind/body split, come from phenomenology. In this trend, the notion of *Dasein,* which literally means "to be here," was introduced and developed by Martin Heidegger[93]. We also find this theme introduced in the work of Ludwig Binswanger, the founder of Dasein Analysis (Daseinanalyse), an approach that synthesizes psychoanalysis and phenomenology. However, unlike Dasein which involves being "thrown into the world," the Self is related to the origins from which it arises.

To become one's true Self is more important than becoming a *Dasein*. Knowing where one comes from is also

[92] See the Glossary: Phenomenology.

[93] Whose history resembles in some respects that of Oedipus, accused for "most unforgivable" conduct.

reflected in the ancient Greek word *Aletheia*[94], usually translated as "truth," but whose literal meaning may be parsed as "that which is not hidden or forgotten." The reader will understand the relevance of this concept in a transgenerational context, as it aligns with the timelessness of the psyche and the unveiling of a past that remains present because it has not been integrated.

Inspired by traditional African practices, the "family constellations" of Bert Hellinger also reflect a phenomenological approach. He explains, "This form of therapy is about developing a specific, fundamental attitude, the phenomenological attitude, characterized by receptiveness in the face of reality. Thanks to this attitude, we are no longer tempted to manipulate the reality which presents itself, either to attenuate it or to accentuate it."[95]

According to Binswanger, the phenomenological approach invites us into this dimension which belongs to our Self—the present, or the *ipse*[96]. Citing Heraclitus and Saint Augustine, Binswanger reminds us that the *ipseity* of the Self involves "searching for our Self within ourselves" or a "return towards one's true Self."

That is why Binswanger distinguishes two ways to practice psychotherapy. "One distances you from yourself in favor of a theoretical fixation [...], the other leads us 'into ourselves' in an anthropological way, meaning that we stay in contact with our most individual and intrinsic present being, which we assume as a creator."[97] For Pierre

---

[94] *Aléthèia* is made up of the particle *"a"* which signifies negation and *Thèia* which signifies forgetfulness, to create the meaning "what is not forgotten".

[95] Bert Hellinger (2010), *À la découverte des constellations familiales*, Jouvence, Bernex-Geneva.

[96] *Ipse* means "Self, in person; himself, herself" and, by extension "in itself, by itself, of itself".

[97] Ludwig Binswanger (1970), *Analyse existentielle et psychanalyse freudienne*, Gallimard, Paris, pp. 227-228.

Fédida, phenomenology renounces "the passionate need to draw conclusions to form one's own opinion or judgment, which is ingrained within us by our intellectual and naturalistic education. The phenomenological attitude commands us to renounce this because it asks us to let the thing itself speak to us."[98]

The hermeneutic of the Self combines the phenomenological approach with the analysis of the Self—the capacity to recognize, behind appearances, the Self that seeks to emerge, as Theseus did for Oedipus. Mixing family tree analysis with this hermeneutic of the Self brings considerable insights and transformations. We saw this for example, when Catherine realized that what she had experienced with her husband, reflected her unconscious relation to her mother. This insight allowed her to make sense of the difficulties experienced in her marriage, and thus to better integrate that part of her story.

Another example from my practice illustrates this association between the hermeneutic of the Self and transgenerational analysis. Mario came to consult because he felt out of place and was experiencing financial difficulties. Since childhood, he had feared possible violence against him, as well as his own aggressive impulses towards these imagined aggressors. He was particularly uncomfortable when he had to cross borders, fearing wrongful imprisonment and accusations, without being able to prove his innocence. An analysis of his family tree led us to a better understanding of the lack of transmission of the stories of his Italian ancestors during the war; their ambivalent relations with the fascist regime, and the change of government that rallied to the coalition—making yesterday's allies today's enemies. All these clarifications helped

---

[98] Pierre Fédida (1970), "Binswanger et l'impossibilité de conclure", preface to the work *Ludwig Binswanger, analyse existentielle et psychanalyse freudienne*, Gallimard, Paris, p. 25.

Mario realize how these unfinished stories had influenced his life. Then, he discovered the life of a great-uncle, a well-known and controversial public figure. He was a representative of the fascist movement in Switzerland, and he had close ties with Italian leaders. At the end of the war, to avoid the local escalation of hatred, the Swiss government had expelled him.

Mario's father had never heard of these important stories, even though they were a part of his own father's youth. Mario was relieved to discover this and to better understand where some of his problems came from. He also made sense of some of the intense conflicts during his adolescence and his ambivalent issues with loyalty and belonging to rival groups. The discovery of what had alienated him unconsciously, enabled him to come back to himself, and to distance himself from ideas and career options that he'd considered definitive until then. From then on, he began to consider what others had advised him to do in the past. In other words, by becoming more himself, he was able to better judge his current situation and imagine new ways to make it evolve.

As this example shows, the therapeutic benefits of transgenerational integration do not depend on beliefs or explanations. Instead of merely judging our experiences at the level of their appearances, we should learn to delve into their meaning, which involves going through and integrating them. By doing so, we acquire life lessons that can be passed on. As I have shown with the myth of Oedipus, if we simply judge him for his symptomatic actions, we miss the deeper meaning of the myth and Sophocles' teachings on transgenerational laws. It is a teaching hidden behind appearances, reserved for those who are worthy of it, and who do not settle for ready-made explanations.

We are here in a direct confrontation with what "is," and not with what should or could be. This way of approaching reality is an alternative to the modern tendency to develop general explanations and to take refuge in metaphysical abstractions. Instead, one should come back to the present moment, to a subjective, personal, and unique experience. Who could have suspected that Catherine's marital difficulties reflected unconscious issues in her relationship with her mother? Who could have predicted that Mario's conflicts mirrored those of his ancestors during the Second World War?

Nicolas Abraham rightly insists on the present dimension in analytical work: "The true place of psychoanalysis is not time, in the sense of discontinuous time, nor the eternal, but rather the living present, *lebendige Gegenwart,* that is, the present in which all the past is revived[99] And "the primary role belongs to the living flow of the present. It is polarized between two protagonists. The world on the one hand and the Ego on the other. In this flow, there is only one entity of coexistence. The Ego itself lives in alienation."[100] Since unfinished stories of our ancestors do not belong to the past but are still represented today, we must also position ourselves in this present moment and engage with the part of us that is always present—our real Self. It is by being more present, and knowing ourselves, that we can heal from our hidden heritage.

---

[99] Nicolas Abraham (1999), *Rythmes; de la philosophie, de la psychanalyse, de la poésie*, Aubier, Paris, p. 167.

[100] Nicolas Abraham and Maria Torok, *The Shell and the Kernel: Renewals of Psychoanalysis*, 1994, University of Chicago Press.

Conclusion

With the therapeutic examples and with the transgenerational analysis of Oedipus' myth, we have been able to understand how symptoms and acting out can manifest an unconscious heritage. Between the *Personae* who perpetuates a lack of integration and the *nirvana style* that replays them, alienations spread from one generation to the next. When we know what to look out for, we can recognize the presence of a true Self awaiting to arise behind the symptoms. The same way Theseus welcomes Oedipus, as a therapist would—going beyond appearances.

It was a true discovery[101] that came with challenges to realize how similar principles apply in both contemporary transgenerational therapy and in Oedipus' myth, even though they're separated by more than two thousand years. This parallel shed light on both ancient and contemporary knowledge and it is from this enlarged perspective that I have attempted to define what I call: *transgenerational integration.*

With transgenerational integration, Depth Psychology can further develop its promising initial research without turning its back on ancient cultures. Contrary to modern reductionism, by renewing and reconnecting with traditional forms of knowledge, Depth Psychology can supersede the usual sterile dogmatic conflicts found in most modern schools of thought.

Instead of restricting our field of vision and multiplying therapeutic specialization (which is what is happening nowadays), transgenerational analysis invites us to return

---

[101] A discovery discussed more extensively in *A Model for Healing Family Curses, Oedipus' journey from outcast to hero of Colonus,* Genesis Editions, 2024.

to our roots and get to know ourselves better. The individual who knows themself better will be much more open to others and different ideas and beliefs, without feeling threatened. On the contrary, this person would enrich themself thanks to the diversity of their ideas, without losing their time in vain arguments fed by transferential needs (personal, familial, and cultural). We can inspire ourselves from this glorious Athenian era in which different cultures and religions cohabited intelligently. For Claude Calame, "The Greeks were very comfortable with this diversity of narrative. There is evidence of this in Aristophanes as well as in Euripides, where myths and religious and political practices of the city of Sparta were acted out in Athens."[102] Shouldn't we associate a community's openness of mind with an understanding of its roots, where self-knowledge was not the abstract concept it has become today?

Looking back at the change in civilization in Athens is like discovering a long-forgotten treasure hidden under the dusty cobwebs in the attic of a house that once belonged to our ancestors. Symbolically speaking, the treasure that punctuates Sophocles' works is finding the part of ourselves which were once nearly forgotten, despite the personal and societal symptoms which had urged us to dig a little deeper.

In this new light, Sophocles' play reveals an exceptional therapeutic model that addresses many contemporary questions. This transgenerational interpretation of Oedipus' myth frees us from the limits of our so-called modern culture, which is cut off from its origins and founding myths. It restores a sense of Self which was once almost lost. Such an approach, which broadens our horizons, challenges the modern tendency to oppose new and

---

[102] Claude Calame, Interview published in *La Grèce et ses dieux*, Le Point, July 2016, Paris.

ancient knowledge, highlighting instead the necessity to know our elders better and to assimilate our origins. Many forms of therapy that claim to be more "modern and innovative" than others, repeat the same error as our civilization by ignoring and denigrating older knowledge without considering how to renew and adapt it to our contemporary world. Transgenerational integration offers an alternative to this modern tendency where the individual tries to free themself from their unconscious transgenerational heritage by cutting themself off from their roots and, in doing so, loses themself.

This new interpretation of Oedipus' myth might be challenging to grasp for those unfamiliar with transgenerational laws. To reconnect with Sophocles' traditional teaching, we must go back to the source, while rejecting certain prejudices present in our modern culture. It is a journey that I have found myself on more than once, in order to bring out the main transgenerational dimensions of the myth. Ultimately, this new interpretation appears so obvious that it's hard not to question the widespread neglect of transgenerational understanding in our culture today. Indeed, once we are aware of what is transmitted between generations, it is no longer possible to overlook Sophocles' teachings. That is why, in my view, the discovery of a transgenerational structure underlying Sophocles' masterpieces is a major finding—akin to the discovery of the *Rosetta Stone*[103]. Sophocles' play presents an ideal model of transgenerational healing, as relevant today as it was then. This symbolic model is highly valuable for those who really want to learn about transgenerational laws.

---

[103] The *Rosetta stone* is a granite fragment on which the same text was written in three different languages: in hieroglyphics, demotic Egyptian and the Greek alphabet. This allowed hieroglyphics to finally be deciphered and understood.

Integrating our prehistory

The development of the Self and its emancipation from alienation arise from the same transformation that Oedipus goes through. Big or small, these rebirths reorganize our relationship with the world: certain truths are revealed, freeing us from the consequences of previous misunderstandings. Since it addresses an extreme form of alienation and healing, Oedipus' rebirth provides an ideal holistic therapeutical model.

We do not come into the world independently of our parents and their families, who themselves are influenced by the culture they live in. Furthermore, cutting us off from our origins would amount to losing ourselves in a superficial way of life. It is therefore essential to integrate these origins, to achieve a transformation that is more qualitative than quantitative—a transformation to become oneself. Those who defend themselves against their unconscious legacies by erecting egocentric defenses sever their bonds with their roots, their real Self, and with other individuals who have connected with themselves. They might amplify the impact of their alienations on their entourage and their descendants. To free oneself from one's alienations does not depend on putting in place new resistances, rational explanations, or ego reinforcement. On the contrary, by integrating its origins the person enters a fertile continuum.

Instead of nurturing this modern fantasy of cutting oneself off from one's roots to feel better, the transgenerational approach seeks the symbolic integration of these roots. Alan Watts[104] describes the difference between these two approaches. "For every individual is a unique manifestation of the Whole, as every branch is a particular outreach of the tree. To manifest individuality, every

---

[104] Alan Watts (1966), *The Book: On the Taboo Against Knowing Who You Are*, Vintage Cookery Books.

branch must have a connection with the tree, just as our independently moving and differentiated fingers must have a connection with the whole body. The point, which can hardly be repeated too often, is that differentiation and separation are not the same thing. The head and the feet are different, but not separate, and though man is not connected to the universe by exactly the same physical relation as branch to tree or feet to head, he is nonetheless connected..."

Reconnecting with our origins and becoming aware of how our ancestors experienced their existence, as well as their unfinished stories, seems to be an important step in personal and therapeutic development. Indeed, anyone seeking to know themself better and to answer the question *"Who am I?"* may find some answers by exploring the history of their family tree. As the Ancients explained, our true Self may emerge as inherited alienations are brought to light. Therapeutic experience has shown the extent to which transgenerational integration enhances self-awareness. Indeed, to know oneself is as important today as it was in ancient Greece.

As I tried to show throughout the book, going beyond appearances and unveiling the presence of hidden heritages requires an open, symbolic, and holistic approach. Along with its therapeutic benefits, this approach allows us to assimilate valuable heritages and ancient wisdom, such as the teachings found in Sophocles' masterpieces on Oedipus.

Finally, as seen with the therapeutical examples, transgenerational analysis fosters a dialogue between the inner psychological world and the outer world. As such, it reflects universal therapeutic principles that have remained true throughout the ages and concern us all, yesterday as well as today.

Appendix

Summary of *Oedipus the King*

One day, during Oedipus' reign as king of Thebes, his subjects gather outside the palace to ask for his help. A devastating plague is ravaging the kingdom and rendering the crops, the livestock, the men, and women of the city barren. Oedipus responds that he too is troubled by these circumstances and that he is determined to heal his kingdom. He reveals that he has already sent Creon, the brother of his wife Jocasta, to consult the oracle about the problem.

Upon his return, Creon conveys the oracle's message: the plague is the result of the unsolved murder of the former King of Thebes, Laius. Oedipus vows to uncover the truth about this crime and to punish the perpetrator. He then summons Tiresias, the blind seer who possesses the gift of clairvoyance. At first, the seer refuses to tell Oedipus what he knows, fearing it will only bring further tragedy. Angered, Oedipus threatens Tiresias and forces him to speak. Against his will, Tiresias gives in and reveals that Oedipus himself is the murderer he seeks; a man who is both brother and father to his own children, and both son and husband of the woman who brought him into the world.

Oedipus is unable to accept such a revelation and instead suspects that Tiresias and Creon are conspiring to usurp his throne. Jocasta tries to calm the rising conflict by downplaying Tiresias's words, arguing that: no one is capable of correctly interpreting the oracles without the risk of making a mistake. As proof, she cites the prophecy that Laius would die at the hands of his own son, when in fact, Laius was reportedly killed by highwaymen at the crossroads of Delphi and Daulis, according to a servant who escaped the scene.

However, Jocasta's arguments fail to calm Oedipus. He recalls a rumor that surfaced when a drunken man at a festival claimed that Oedipus was not the true son of Polybius and Merope, the king and queen of Corinth. Though his parents denied the allegation, Oedipus was so troubled by the accusation that he sought answers from the oracle. Instead of resolving his doubts, the oracle prophesied that he would marry his mother, bring a curse upon his descendants, and kill his own father. Horrified, Oedipus fled towards Thebes to avoid this fate, hoping to protect those he believed to be his parents. Along the way a man started a fight with him about who had the right of way at a crossroads. In the ensuing struggle, Oedipus killed the attacker and several members of his entourage, except for one servant who managed to escape.

Determined to uncover the truth, Oedipus orders that the escaped servant who saw the highwaymen that killed Laius be found. At that moment, a messenger from Corinth arrives and announces that King Polybius has died from illness and old age. This news comforts Oedipus, who believes that he has thereby escaped the prophecy: he did not kill his father. However, the messenger then reveals that Polybius was not Oedipus's biological father and that his permanent fear was unfounded. The messenger himself had received the infant Oedipus from the hands of a shepherd of the house of Laius on the slopes of Mount Cithaeron. Instead of leaving the child hanging by his feet, to be killed by wild beasts as ordered by King Laius, the shepherd took pity on the child and gave him to the messenger, who then gave the baby to the childless king and queen of Corinth. They decided to name him Oedipus on account of his swollen feet after he had been hung from a tree.

In the face of these revelations, Jocasta is troubled and asks Oedipus not to continue his investigation. But Oedipus is determined to learn the truth of his origins. He believes that, as he was born in Thebes, he has a right to know whether he is of noble birth. He cannot understand why Jocasta would ask him to stop unless she fears his origins are humble. Convinced that he is a "son of Fortune," Oedipus feels no shame

The servant who witnessed Laius's death is finally brought in. Immediately, the messenger from Corinth recognizes him as the man who handed over the infant Oedipus. Under pressure, the servant admits that the child was indeed the son of Laius and Jocasta, condemned to die on Mount Cithaeron because of the prophecy that he would kill his parents. However, the servant had not been able to carry out the order and instead gave the child to the messenger from Corinth

When he discovers his true history, Oedipus realizes that in spite of himself he has indeed committed parricide and incest as the oracle had predicted. Already in a state of shock over this revelation, he then receives word that Jocasta has just hung herself in her room. Oedipus rushes there, and in a fit of suffering, he stabs out his eyes with the broaches that held together the robes of the woman who was both his mother and his wife.

In his state of turmoil, Oedipus demands to be sent into exile and abandoned to his cursed fate. However, Creon decides to consult the oracle to learn what should be done.

Summary of Oedipus at Colonus

Accompanied by his daughter Antigone, Oedipus arrives close to Colonus, weary from his journey in exile. As soon as they settle, a local resident asks them to leave the area, explaining that it is a sacred place where human presence is forbidden. This announcement brings joy to

Oedipus, as it signifies the end of his long, painful journey. He confides to Antigone that the oracle had also foretold that he would find refuge in this sacred place home to the Eumenides (or Furies), and that if he settled there, he would become a benefactor to those who welcomed him.

Oedipus requests that Theseus, the king of the land, be informed that his arrival could bring great fortune in exchange for a small act of kindness. While waiting for Theseus, the elders of Colonus try to persuade Oedipus to leave, fearing that his presence might defile the sacred space. It is then that the second daughter of Oedipus, Ismene, arrives unexpectedly. She announces that war is imminent between her two brothers, Polynices and Eteocles, who both lay claim to the throne of Thebes. Ismene also informs them that the Thebans, having consulted a new oracle, now seek to capture Oedipus, believing that his presence or even his remains will bring them victory. Though they wish to secure him, they do not intend to allow him to return to Thebes; planning to keep him near the border only. Forewarned of the true intentions of the Thebans, Oedipus curses his sons who, once again, value the crown of Thebes more than their father's well-being. They refused to support him when he sought exile and failed to defend him when, desperate, he was condemned to it.

Theseus arrives to meet with Oedipus. After exchanging a few words of mutual respect, Theseus declares that he knows well what it means to live in exile, having experienced it for himself; as a simple mortal man, he is no more able to control the future than Oedipus. Therefore, he grants Oedipus' request for hospitality and promises to protect him. Relieved, Oedipus promises that, before he dies, he will entrust Theseus with a secret that will assure that his people's prosperity.

At this point Creon makes an appearance and attempts to persuade Oedipus to return to Thebes. However, thanks to Ismene's warning, Oedipus sees through Creon's deceit and accuses him of trying to manipulate him with false promises. Dropping the pretense, Creon orders his guards to kidnap Antigone and Ismene, provoking outrage among the people of Colonus. Angry, Creon threatens to seize Oedipus himself, accusing him of being a criminal. Oedipus replies that he is innocent of the crimes of which he is accused, that he is the victim of what the gods had decided for him before he was even born. He admits that his marriage to Jocasta was unlawful but insists that it occurred unknowingly. He then turns on Creon, accusing him of lacking conscience and compassion, and for continuing to torment him despite his innocence. Witnessing this confrontation, Theseus honors his promise, rescues Oedipus's daughters, and drives off Creon's men.

Later, Polynices appears, seeking his father's support in his conflict with Eteocles for the throne of Thebes. But Oedipus explains that he is no longer the person they knew, declaring that to him Polynices and Eteocles are not his sons anymore. He tells Polynices that he cannot lift the curse that hangs over them, nor can he alter the destiny they have brought upon themselves.

At that point a great commotion is heard—it is the thunder of Zeus, the last call for Oedipus' earthly life. Oedipus sends for Theseus to accompany him in this last moment of his life. He promises to reveal to Theseus the secret that will ensure the prosperity of his kingdom but insists that Theseus must never forget the name of Oedipus.

A messenger who followed the two men from a distance reports to Ismene and Antigone what he witnessed. The thunder of the god summoned Oedipus while Theseus covered his eyes, dazzled by the divine presence. Oedipus's death remains shrouded in mystery, perhaps raised up by the gods or swallowed by the earth. Be that as it may, when Theseus returns to Antigone and Ismene, he announces that they no longer need to grieve because they now benefit from the protection of the dead. Before dying, Oedipus had thus kept his promise and delivered to Theseus the secret that would guarantee the prosperity of his kingdom.

Glossary

Alienation - The *Id*, the *Ego* and the *Superego* - Phenomenology - Positivism – Knowing one's Self

Alienation

The verb "to alienate"[105] appears (in French) in law (1265) as a borrowing from the Latin *alienure*, "to render other" or "to render strange", derived from *alienus*, "other", itself derived from *alius* (alias, alibi). Later, the verb "to alienate" came to mean, "to drive someone crazy".

"Alienation" acquires the definition of "madness" in 1811. In the 20th century, it took on a new usage, being chosen as the translation of the German *Entfremdung*, an important philosophical concept for Hegel, and then for Marx, "the state in which a human being seems detached from himself, turned away from his true awareness by socio-economic conditions." The success of this concept led to the use of the word and certain derivatives in a vaguer sense: "a human being's loss of authenticity", bringing together the 18th century's popular theme of the harmful effects of life in society and the 19th century's theme of the exploitation of man by man.

The Id, the Ego and the Superego

Freud distinguished three related aspects of the function of the psyche: the *Id*, the *Ego*, and the *Superego*. The Id refers to the vital forces in a person, his impulses or his libido. It neither recognizes norms (prohibitions or obligations) nor reality (time and space) and is ruled by the

---

105 From the dictionary of the "History of the French language", *Le Robert*, Paris, p. 45.

pleasure principle, always looking for the immediate satisfaction of its needs.

The Ego is the part of the psyche that manages the conditions necessary for the satisfaction of impulses, while considering the demands of reality. It controls the demands of the Id and the Superego, and is at the same time conscious, preconscious, and unconscious. The Ego develops within the context of the processes of integration and/or repression.

The Superego dominates the ego and imposes itself upon it. It is a sort of moral structure defining what is good or bad. The Superego is severe and cruel, often in the form of injunctions that unconsciously constrain the individual. A critical agent, basically unconscious most of the time, the Superego decides which impulses to repress when it judges them to be unacceptable.

Phenomenology

For phenomenology, Being comes first. First, we are, we exist, then we are one way or another. Thus, phenomenology distinguishes "Being" from "beings". Being is the very fact of existing. "Beings," on the other hand, designate things as we usually relate to them, not primarily with concerns for their existence, but for what they represent as such. In phenomenology, the true meaning of beings can only be found in the realm of Being.

Merleau-Ponty illustrates the relationship between Being and a being by means of the following analogy: light makes it possible for us to perceive objects in a room. For him, the act of unveiling Being is similar to lighting a room. The light enables us to see, however it is not, itself, an object to be seen. Without light we could not perceive an object, in the same way as without Being, there would not be any beings.

Phenomenology "makes something seen by reference to what it is in its Being". It seeks to unveil the very Being of things, so that their true meaning appears to us. Heidegger asks: "What is it that phenomenology lets be seen"? [...] Manifestly it is something that does not show itself at first and for the most part, something that is concealed, in contrast to what at first and for the most part does show itself. [...] What remains concealed in an exceptional way, or what falls back and is covered up again, or shows itself only in a distorted way, is not this or that being but rather, as we have shown in our foregoing observations, the Being of beings."[106]

In contrast to phenomenology, metaphysics inquiries into the being as a being, into things as they are. That is, it determines what the beings are in and of themselves and not in their relationship to Being. "To the extent that constantly represents only the being as a being, metaphysics does not include Being itself in its thinking... A thought that contemplates the truth of Being can no longer be satisfied with metaphysics; nonetheless it has nothing against metaphysics", however, it tries to go beyond metaphysics.

Positivism

Auguste Comte (1789-1857) introduced positivism as a new approach to the social sciences. For him, nothing makes sense apart from objective science. Scientists should collect observations without prejudices to gather up the facts from which one can abstract generalizations.

This approach attempts to first *describe* reality, so that it can then *predict* its evolution, using scientific laws. The idea is that if you can predict, then you will be able to *control*. In this way science should be able to explain everything within an abstract system of logical theories. Too idealistic in certain aspects of its philosophy, positivism

---

[106] Martin Heidegger, "Being and time", in Basic Writings, 1992, Harper, San Francisco, p. 82.

has sometimes been pushed to extremes which have been called "scientism."

Even though the limits of logical positivism had been demonstrated, this causal and rationalistic way of thinking continues to pass for a scientific approach. As such, it has invaded the field of social sciences, which are anxious about their scientific-ness. Yet its limitations are significant. The principal criticism consists of the mistakenness of the idea that it could be possible to observe the world without prejudices or filters. If a researcher were truly working without any pre-judgements, how would it be able to extract from the massive amount of data those elements that can be organized into a scientific law? He must necessarily rely upon a set of assumptions in order to organize his observation. These assumptions do not come out of nowhere; they evolve from a confrontation between that which is already known and that which is still unknown. In truth, the supposed neutrality of the observer is neither possible nor desirable if science is going to evolve.

Under examination the positivist criterion of objectivity reveals itself to be pure ideology. This becomes particularly flagrant when it is a matter of studying the psyche where it is impossible to ignore unconscious predetermined bias. Today, scientific objectivity in human sciences should be considered a myth.

Knowing one's Self

Knowledge about one's Self takes on its true meaning in the present. To understand it properly, we must differentiate between Self-knowledge and knowledge about oneself. The latter designates information held about oneself, perceived from an outside, or objective, point of view. In this case, a woman can say "I am a fussy person" and believe that she knows herself, when rather, she is only making a judgement on herself. This type of knowledge "about" oneself is often found in a positivist discourse that uses representations which we are meant to believe.

Self-knowledge is another form of knowledge entirely. It is not abstract, but alive, something that is felt, and which resonates within our lives in the here and now. It is global, rational, irrational, and emotional. It concerns existence itself, Being rather than Having.

Bibliography

ABRAHAM Nicolas and TOROK Maria (1987), *The Shell and the Kernel: Renewals of Psychoanalysis*, 1994, University of Chicago Press.

ABRAHAM Nicolas (1999), *Rythmes ; de la philosophie, de la psychanalyse, de la poésie*, Aubier, Paris.

AUSLOSS Guy (1980), « Œdipe et sa famille, ou les secrets sont faits pour être agis » dans *Dialogue*, n°70, AFCCC, Paris.

BETTELHEIM Bruno (1976), *The Uses of Enchantment*, Random House, New York.

BINSWANGER Ludwig (1955-1957), *Analyse existentielle et psychanalyse freudienne*, Gallimard, 1970, Paris.

CAMPBELL Joseph (1999), *Transformation of Myth Through Time*, Harper Perennia, New York.

CANAULT Nina (1998), *Comment paye-t-on les fautes de ses ancêtres*, Desclée de Brouwer, Paris.

CORNIOU Marine, « Nos états d'âmes modifient notre ADN », *Sciences et Vie*, 1110 (03/2010), Paris.

DEVEREUX Georges (1953), "Why Oedipus killed Laius: a note on the complementary Oedipus complex" in *International Journal of psycho-analysis*, n°34, Wiley, NY.

DEVEREUX Georges (1977), *Essais d'ethnopsychiatrie générale*, Gallimard, Paris.

DODDS Eric R. (1951*), The Greeks and the Irrational*, University of California Press.

DUMAS Didier (2000*), Et l'enfant créa le père*, Hachette Littérature, Paris.

DUMAS Didier (2001), *La Bible et ses fantômes*, Desclée de Brouwer, Paris.

ELIADE Mircea, *Rites and Symbols of Initiation* (Birth and Rebirth), Harvill Press, 1958, London.

EURIDIPES (1973), *Les Phéniciennes*, Les Belles Lettres, Paris.

FERENCZI Sándor (1908), « Transfert et introjection », in *Psychanalyse I*, Payot, Paris, (1968).

FRAIBERG Selma (1980), *Clinical Studies in Infant Mental Health*, Basic Books, New York.

FREUD Sigmund (1920), *Beyond the Pleasure Principle*, Norton, NY.

FREUD Sigmund, *Moses and Monotheism, three essays*, Hogarth Press, (1878), London.

FREUD Sigmund, *Civilization and its Discontent*, Norton & Company, 1961, New York.

FREUD Sigmund (1999), *Conférences d'introduction à la psychanalyse*, Gallimard, Paris.

FROMM Erich (1951), *The Forgotten Language; an introduction to the understanding of dreams, fairy tales, and myths*, 1988, Random House, New York.

GAILLARD T. Tony (2024), *A Model for Healing Family Curses, Oedipus' journey from outcast to hero of Colonus,* Genesis Editions, Geneva.

GAILLARD T. Tony and C. Michael SMITH, Olivier DOUVILLE, Pierre RAMAUT, Elisabeth HOROWITZ, Iona MILLER, Myron ESHOWSKY (2020) *Shamanism, Ancestors and Transgenerational Therapy*, Genesis Editions, Geneva.

GAILLARD T. Thierry (2021), *Thérapie transgénérationnelle et psychogenèse du sujet, Principes et fondamentaux*, Genesis Editions, Geneva.

GAILLARD T. Thierry (2024), *Intégrer ses héritages transgénérationnels, Une synthèse des pratiques anciennes et contemporaines*, Genesis Editions, Geneva.

GAILLARD T. Thierry (2012), *L'autre Œdipe,* De Freud à Sophocle, Genesis Editions, Geneva.

GAILLARD T. Thierry (2013), *Sophocle thérapeute, la guérison d'Œdipe à Colone*, Genesis Editions, Geneva.

GRIMBERT Philippe, (2012), *Secret*, Granta Books, NY.

HEIDEGGER Martin (1978), *Being and Time*, 1927, Wiley-Blackwell, NY.

HELLINGER Bert (2010), *Á la découverte des constellations familiales*, Jouvence, Bernex-Geneva.

JUNG Carl Gustav, *The Collected Works of C. G. Jung*, Routledge, 2015, NY.

JUNG Carl Gustav, (1966), *Memories, Dream, Reflections*, Vintage, NY.

MIJOLLA de Alain (1981), *Les visiteurs du moi*, Les Belles Lettres, Paris.

MOREL-FERLA Denise (2015), *Les ressources créatives des familles d'artistes*, Ecodition, Geneva.

NAOURI Aldo (1985), *Une place pour le père*, Seuil, Paris.

RESWEBER Jean-Paul (1996), *Le transfert : enjeux cliniques, pédagogiques et culturels*, l'Harmattan, Paris.

RICHARD Michel (1998), *Les courants de la psychologie*, Chroniques Sociales, Lyon.

RILKE Rainer Maria (1929), *Les cahiers de Malte Laurids Brigge*, Seuil 1966, Paris.

ROSS John-Munder (1982), « Oedipus revisited, Laius and the *Laius complex*», dans *Psychoanalytic Studies of the Child*, vol. 37, Yale University Press.

ROUCHY Jean-Claude (editor) (2001), *La psychanalyse avec Nicolas Abraham et Maria Torok*, Érès, Paris.

SCHÜTZENBERGER Anne Ancelin (1998), *The Ancestor Syndrome: Transgenerational Psychotherapy and the Hidden Links in the Family Tree*, Routledge, London.

SELLAM Salomon (2007), *Le syndrome du gisant*, Bérangel, Saint-André-de-Sagonis.

SICHROVSKY Peter (1989), *Born Guilty: Children of Nazi Families*, Basic Books, NY.

SOPHOCLES, *The Three Theban Plays*, translated by Robert Fagles, Penguin Classics, 1984, New York.

TISSERON Serge (1996), *Secrets de famille, mode d'emploi*, Ramsay, Collection Marabout, Paris.

TISSERON Serge (editor) (1995), *Le psychisme à l'épreuve des générations : clinique du fantôme*, Dunod, Paris.

TISSERON Serge (1992), *Tintin et les secrets de famille*, Aubier, Paris.

TOLLE Eckhart, (2004), *The Power of the Now*, Namaste Publishing, Vancouver.

VERNANT Jean-Pierre and VIDAL-NAQUET Pierre (1994), *Œdipe et ses mythes*, Complexe, Brussels.

WATTS Alan (1966), *The Book: On the Taboo Against Knowing Who You Are*, Vintage Cookery Books.

WOLYNN Marc (2016), *It didn't start with you*, Viking, New York.

www.ingramcontent.com/pod-product-compliance
Ingram Content Group UK Ltd.
Pitfield, Milton Keynes, MK11 3LW, UK
UKHW022013260726
13994UKWH00006B/2441